THE

BIBLE

PROMISE

BOOK®

THE
BIBLE
PROMISE
BOOK®

Discipleship
Edition

King James Version

BARBOUR BOOKS
An Imprint of Barbour Publishing, Inc.

© 2018 by Barbour Publishing, Inc.

Topic introductions written and scripture compiled by Ed Strauss.

Print ISBN 978-1-68322-374-0

eBook Editions:
Adobe Digital Edition (.epub) 978-1-68322-661-1
Kindle and MobiPocket Edition (.prc) 978-1-68322-662-8

All scripture quotations are taken from the King James Version of the Bible.

Published by Barbour Books, an imprint of Barbour Publishing, Inc., 1810 Barbour Drive, Uhrichsville, Ohio 44683, www.barbourbooks.com.

Our mission is to inspire the world with the life-changing message of the Bible.

Member of the
Evangelical Christian
Publishers Association

Printed in the United States of America.

CONTENTS

INTRODUCTION

GOD'S PROMISES FOR THE DISCIPLE'S HEART

This Bible promise book has a special focus on discipleship. If you have accepted Christ as your Savior and Lord and are seeking to obey Him, you are His disciple. This book was written to help you in that high calling.

It's important to understand that you serve God out of gratitude for what He has done for you. Many Christians misunderstand discipleship. They think that although Jesus' blood paid for their salvation initially, once they are saved, it's then up to *them* to do good works to try to hang on to their salvation. To this, Paul asked, "Are ye so foolish? having begun in the Spirit, are ye now made perfect by the flesh?" (Galatians 3:3).

When Jesus cried out on the cross, "It is finished" (John 19:30), He uttered the Greek word *Tetelestai*, used to describe a debt that had been paid in full. It's your job to simply receive the gift that Christ offers, then to follow Him as His disciple in gratitude for what He's done. The same grace of God that saved you will now work in your life daily to enable you to live for Him (Titus 2:11–12).

Our prayer is that this book will help you walk in the grace and love of God as you strive to be His disciple day after day.

1. SALVATION

We're short-lived, earthbound mortals, but God is an infinite, immortal, transcendent Being. We're pitiful sinners, but God is holy, "dwelling in the light which no man can approach unto" (1 Timothy 6:16). But we need to come into His presence to have eternal life. So the question is, How *can* we approach Him? How *can* we come into His presence?

Jesus said, "No man cometh unto the Father, but by me" (John 14:6).

People in the Bible were constantly asking Him, "Good Master, what shall I do that I may inherit eternal life?" (Mark 10:17), or "Master, what shall I do to inherit eternal life?" (Luke 10:25). You notice that they thought doing good deeds made them worthy. They hoped Jesus' answer would be something like, "Give alms to the poor," or "Don't steal"—something they were already doing.

But when they asked Jesus, "What shall we do, that we might work the works of God?" Jesus answered, "This is the work of God, that ye believe on him whom he hath sent" (John 6:28–29). Years later, a similar conversation took place. A Philippian jailer asked Paul and Silas, "Sirs, what must I do to be saved?" and they answered, "Believe on the Lord Jesus Christ, and thou shalt be saved" (Acts 16:30–31).

The answer is just that simple: believe on Jesus.

Jesus answereth again, and saith unto them, Children,
how hard is it for them that trust in riches to enter into
the kingdom of God! It is easier for a camel to go through
the eye of a needle, than for a rich man to enter into the
kingdom of God. And they were astonished out of measure,
saying among themselves, Who then can be saved? And
Jesus looking upon them saith, With men it is impossible,
but not with God: for with God all things are possible.

MARK 10:24–27

But as many as received him, to them gave he power to
become the sons of God, even to them that believe on his
name.

JOHN 1:12

For God so loved the world, that he gave his only begotten
Son, that whosoever believeth in him should not perish, but
have everlasting life.

JOHN 3:16

He that believeth on the Son hath everlasting life: and he
that believeth not the Son shall not see life; but the wrath
of God abideth on him.

JOHN 3:36

All that the Father giveth me shall come to me; and him
that cometh to me I will in no wise cast out.

JOHN 6:37

And I give unto them eternal life; and they shall never perish, neither shall any man pluck them out of my hand.

JOHN 10:28

∞

Then he called for a light, and sprang in, and came trembling, and fell down before Paul and Silas. . .and said, Sirs, what must I do to be saved? And they said, Believe on the Lord Jesus Christ, and thou shalt be saved, and thy house.

ACTS 16:29–31

∞

A man is not justified by the works of the law, but by the faith of Jesus Christ. . .for by the works of the law shall no flesh be justified.

GALATIANS 2:16

∞

And because ye are sons, God hath sent forth the Spirit of his Son into your hearts, crying, Abba, Father.

GALATIANS 4:6

∞

For by grace are ye saved through faith; and that not of yourselves: it is the gift of God: not of works, lest any man should boast.

EPHESIANS 2:8–9

∞

That Christ may dwell in your hearts by faith.

EPHESIANS 3:17

Being confident of this very thing, that he which hath begun a good work in you will perform it until the day of Jesus Christ.

PHILIPPIANS 1:6

Who hath saved us, and called us with an holy calling, not according to our works, but according to his own purpose and grace, which was given us in Christ Jesus before the world began.

2 TIMOTHY 1:9

Not by works of righteousness which we have done, but according to his mercy he saved us, by the washing of regeneration, and renewing of the Holy Ghost.

TITUS 3:5

He that hath the Son hath life; and he that hath not the Son of God hath not life. These things have I written unto you that believe on the name of the Son of God; that ye may know that ye have eternal life, and that ye may believe on the name of the Son of God.

1 JOHN 5:12–13

2. GOD'S MERCY AND FORGIVENESS

Many scriptures *proclaim* the forgiveness and mercy of the Lord, but the passages that best *show* these attributes of God are Psalm 51 and 2 Samuel 12:9, 13.

In Psalm 51, King David's heart is laid bare. He had sinned grievously, committing adultery with Bathsheba, then arranging to have her husband killed so he could take her as his own, and God had called him on it. This psalm is filled with raw emotion and honest confession—but the most outstanding thing about it is the great faith David has in God's mercy.

According to the Law, adulterers and murderers were to be executed. There was no provision for these sins as there was for fornication or manslaughter (Deuteronomy 22:22–29; Numbers 35:16–25). But David cried out, trusting that God *would* forgive him—and God *did* (2 Samuel 12:9–13). For three thousand years, believers who have sinned have found refuge in this psalm, saying, "If God could forgive David, He can forgive me."

David began by praying, "Have mercy upon me, O God, according to thy lovingkindness: according unto the multitude of thy tender mercies blot out my transgressions. Wash me throughly from mine iniquity, and cleanse me from my sin." But he finished by confidently requesting, "Make me to hear joy and gladness," and "Restore unto me the joy of thy salvation" (Psalm 51:1–2, 8, 12).

The Lord is longsuffering, and of great mercy, forgiving iniquity and transgression.

Numbers 14:18

Know therefore that the Lord thy God, he is God, the faithful God, which keepeth covenant and mercy with them that love him and keep his commandments.

Deuteronomy 7:9

Withhold not thou thy tender mercies from me, O Lord: let thy lovingkindness and thy truth continually preserve me.

Psalm 40:11

Hear me, O Lord; for thy lovingkindness is good: turn unto me according to the multitude of thy tender mercies.

Psalm 69:16

The Lord is merciful and gracious, slow to anger, and plenteous in mercy. He will not always chide: neither will he keep his anger for ever. He hath not dealt with us after our sins; nor rewarded us according to our iniquities. For as the heaven is high above the earth, so great is his mercy toward them that fear him. As far as the east is from the west, so far hath he removed our transgressions from us. Like as a father pitieth his children, so the Lord pitieth them that fear him. For he knoweth our frame; he remembereth that we are dust.

Psalm 103:8–14

I will mention the lovingkindnesses of the LORD, and the praises of the LORD, according to all that the LORD hath bestowed on us, and the great goodness toward the house of Israel, which he hath bestowed on them according to his mercies, and according to the multitude of his lovingkindnesses.

ISAIAH 63:7

The LORD hath appeared of old unto me, saying, Yea, I have loved thee with an everlasting love: therefore with lovingkindness have I drawn thee.

JEREMIAH 31:3

For I desired mercy, and not sacrifice; and the knowledge of God more than burnt offerings.

HOSEA 6:6

Who is a God like unto thee, that pardoneth iniquity, and passeth by the transgression of the remnant of his heritage? he retaineth not his anger for ever, because he delighteth in mercy. He will turn again, he will have compassion upon us; he will subdue our iniquities; and thou wilt cast all their sins into the depths of the sea.

MICAH 7:18–19

For I knew that thou art a gracious God, and merciful, slow to anger, and of great kindness, and repentest thee of the evil.

JONAH 4:2

Having predestinated us unto the adoption of children by Jesus Christ to himself, according to the good pleasure of his will, to the praise of the glory of his grace, wherein he hath made us accepted in the beloved. In whom we have redemption through his blood, the forgiveness of sins, according to the riches of his grace.

EPHESIANS 1:5–7

But God, who is rich in mercy, for his great love wherewith he loved us, even when we were dead in sins, hath quickened us together with Christ.

EPHESIANS 2:4–5

Let us therefore come boldly unto the throne of grace, that we may obtain mercy, and find grace to help in time of need.

HEBREWS 4:16

For I will be merciful to their unrighteousness, and their sins and their iniquities will I remember no more.

HEBREWS 8:12

Mercy rejoiceth against judgment.

JAMES 2:13

If we confess our sins, he is faithful and just to forgive us our sins, and to cleanse us from all unrighteousness.

1 JOHN 1:9

Behold, what manner of love the Father hath bestowed upon us, that we should be called the sons of God.

1 JOHN 3:1

3. FAITH AND WORKS

Paul says, "For by grace are ye saved through faith. . .not of works" (Ephesians 2:8–9), but James asks, "Though a man say he hath faith, and have not works. . .can faith save him?" (James 2:14). Paul says, "Faith was reckoned to Abraham for righteousness" (Romans 4:9), but James asks, "Was not Abraham our father justified by works?" and adds that "by works was faith made perfect" (James 2:21–22).

Many Christians therefore conclude that Paul and James contradict each other. But a closer look at the scriptures shows that Paul too preached the necessity of good works. You're saved by grace alone, but if you've truly received the Spirit of Christ, good works will be sure to follow.

Paul wrote that the same grace of God that saves you will also teach you to live a godly life. "For the grace of God that bringeth salvation hath appeared to all men, teaching us that, denying ungodliness and worldly lusts, we should live soberly, righteously, and godly" (Titus 2:11–12).

Peter and James preached the same Gospel as Paul. When referring to Jews and Gentiles, Peter (speaking for James as well) declared, "God. . .put no difference between us and them, purifying their hearts by faith. . . . But we believe that through the grace of the LORD Jesus Christ we shall be saved, even as they" (Acts 15:8–9, 11).

Bring forth therefore fruits meet for repentance.

MATTHEW 3:8

If ye love me, keep my commandments.

JOHN 14:15

He that hath my commandments, and keepeth them, he it is that loveth me: and he that loveth me shall be loved of my Father, and I will love him, and will manifest myself to him.

JOHN 14:21

Whereupon, O king Agrippa, I was not disobedient unto the heavenly vision: but shewed. . .that they should repent and turn to God, and do works meet for repentance.

ACTS 26:19–20

And if by grace, then is it no more of works: otherwise grace is no more grace. But if it be of works, then it is no more grace: otherwise work is no more work.

ROMANS 11:6

I therefore, the prisoner of the Lord, beseech you that ye walk worthy of the vocation wherewith ye are called.

EPHESIANS 4:1

For by grace are ye saved through faith; and that not of yourselves: it is the gift of God: not of works, lest any man should boast. For we are his workmanship, created in Christ Jesus unto good works, which God hath before ordained that we should walk in them.

EPHESIANS 2:8–10

∞

That ye might walk worthy of the Lord unto all pleasing, being fruitful in every good work, and increasing in the knowledge of God.

COLOSSIANS 1:10

∞

They profess that they know God; but in works they deny him, being abominable, and disobedient, and unto every good work reprobate.

TITUS 1:16

∞

For the grace of God that bringeth salvation hath appeared to all men, teaching us that, denying ungodliness and worldly lusts, we should live soberly, righteously, and godly, in this present world.

TITUS 2:11–12

∞

[Jesus Christ] gave himself for us, that he might redeem us from all iniquity, and purify unto himself a peculiar people, zealous of good works.

TITUS 2:14

What doth it profit, my brethren, though a man say he hath faith, and have not works? can faith save him? If a brother or sister be naked, and destitute of daily food, and one of you say unto them, Depart in peace, be ye warmed and filled; notwithstanding ye give them not those things which are needful to the body; what doth it profit? Even so faith, if it hath not works, is dead, being alone. Yea, a man may say, Thou hast faith, and I have works: shew me thy faith without thy works, and I will shew thee my faith by my works. Thou believest that there is one God; thou doest well: the devils also believe, and tremble. But wilt thou know, O vain man, that faith without works is dead? Was not Abraham our father justified by works, when he had offered Isaac his son upon the altar? Seest thou how faith wrought with his works, and by works was faith made perfect?

JAMES 2:14–22

∞

He that saith he abideth in him ought himself also so to walk, even as he walked.

1 JOHN 2:6

∞

But be ye doers of the word, and not hearers only, deceiving your own selves. . . . But whoso looketh into the perfect law of liberty, and continueth therein, he being not a forgetful hearer, but a doer of the work, this man shall be blessed in his deed.

JAMES 1:22, 25

4. THE HOLY SPIRIT

The ancient Jews didn't see any division between the Father and the Spirit of God. They understood that the Holy Spirit was an extension of the one true God. The Holy Spirit knows everything that God knows. "The things of God knoweth no man, but the Spirit of God" (1 Corinthians 2:11). God is all-knowing, and so is the Holy Spirit. That's why the Spirit often gives you godly wisdom.

First John 4:8 says, "God is love," and the Holy Spirit is also known for love. When He dwells inside us, "the love of God is shed abroad in our hearts" (Romans 5:5).

And that was the wonderful promise Jesus made to His disciples—including you—that God His Father would send His Holy Spirit to live in your heart (Galatians 4:6), to make you His own son or daughter. When God's Spirit enters your being, you are filled with the life of God and receive eternal life. You are plugged into God.

The Holy Spirit in your heart also guarantees your full salvation, including the resurrection and transformation of your physical body. God says that the Spirit is a deposit to guarantee the full amount of the regeneration that is to come (Ephesians 1:13–14; 4:30).

Except a man be born of water and of the Spirit, he cannot enter into the kingdom of God. That which is born of the flesh is flesh; and that which is born of the Spirit is spirit.

JOHN 3:5–6

∞

But the Comforter, which is the Holy Ghost, whom the Father will send in my name, he shall teach you all things, and bring all things to your remembrance, whatsoever I have said unto you.

JOHN 14:26

∞

Howbeit when he, the Spirit of truth, is come, he will guide you into all truth: for he shall not speak of himself; but whatsoever he shall hear, that shall he speak: and he will shew you things to come.

JOHN 16:13

∞

But ye shall receive power, after that the Holy Ghost is come upon you: and ye shall be witnesses unto me.

ACTS 1:8

∞

And we are his witnesses of these things; and so is also the Holy Ghost, whom God hath given to them that obey him.

ACTS 5:32

∞

He said unto them, Have ye received the Holy Ghost since ye believed? And they said unto him, We have not so much as heard whether there be any Holy Ghost. . . . And when Paul had laid his hands upon them, the Holy Ghost came on them; and they spake with tongues, and prophesied.

ACTS 19:2, 6

There is therefore now no condemnation to them which are in Christ Jesus, who walk not after the flesh, but after the Spirit. For the law of the Spirit of life in Christ Jesus hath made me free from the law of sin and death. . .that the righteousness of the law might be fulfilled in us, who walk not after the flesh, but after the Spirit.

ROMANS 8:1–2, 4

∞

But ye are not in the flesh, but in the Spirit, if so be that the Spirit of God dwell in you. Now if any man have not the Spirit of Christ, he is none of his.

ROMANS 8:9

∞

For as many as are led by the Spirit of God, they are the sons of God.

ROMANS 8:14

∞

The Spirit itself beareth witness with our spirit, that we are the children of God.

ROMANS 8:16

∞

Likewise the Spirit also helpeth our infirmities: for we know not what we should pray for as we ought: but the Spirit itself maketh intercession for us with groanings which cannot be uttered.

ROMANS 8:26

∞

For the kingdom of God is. . .righteousness, and peace, and joy in the Holy Ghost.

ROMANS 14:17

The love of God is shed abroad in our hearts by the Holy Ghost which is given unto us.

ROMANS 5:5

∽

Now the God of hope fill you with all joy and peace in believing, that ye may abound in hope, through the power of the Holy Ghost.

ROMANS 15:13

∽

And because ye are sons, God hath sent forth the Spirit of his Son into your hearts, crying, Abba, Father.

GALATIANS 4:6

∽

But the fruit of the Spirit is love, joy, peace, longsuffering, gentleness, goodness, faith, meekness, temperance: against such there is no law.

GALATIANS 5:22–23

∽

After that ye believed, ye were sealed with that holy Spirit of promise, which is the earnest [deposit] of our inheritance until the redemption of the purchased possession, unto the praise of his glory.

EPHESIANS 1:13–14

∽

And grieve not the holy Spirit of God, whereby ye are sealed unto the day of redemption.

EPHESIANS 4:30

5. LOVING GOD

The instruction to love God was the most important of all the commands God gave. Thus, when a scribe asked Jesus, "Master, which is the great commandment in the law? Jesus said unto him, Thou shalt love the Lord thy God with all thy heart, and with all thy soul, and with all thy mind. This is the first and great commandment" (Matthew 22:36–38).

Moses asked the Israelites, "What doth the LORD thy God require of thee, but. . .to love him, and to serve the LORD thy God with all thy heart and with all thy soul, to keep the commandments of the LORD?" (Deuteronomy 10:12–13). Jesus said that true worshippers "must worship him in spirit and in truth" (John 4:24), so you must love God sincerely from the heart, not merely with your lips. And if you *do* love God sincerely, you'll desire to keep His commands. Jesus said, "If ye love me, keep my commandments" (John 14:15).

The command to love God has direct benefits to you. Not only does it bring God's blessing on your life and protect you from evil, but as you worship God, His Spirit comes over you, permeates you, and transforms you into His image—an image of a loving God. The closer you draw to God, the more you love Him, the more you become like Him.

And thou shalt love the LORD thy God with all thine heart, and with all thy soul, and with all thy might.

DEUTERONOMY 6:5

∞

And now, Israel, what doth the LORD thy God require of thee, but to fear the LORD thy God, to walk in all his ways, and to love him, and to serve the LORD thy God with all thy heart and with all thy soul, to keep the commandments of the LORD, and his statutes, which I command thee this day for thy good?

DEUTERONOMY 10:12–13

∞

Therefore thou shalt love the LORD thy God, and keep his charge, and his statutes, and his judgments, and his commandments, alway.

DEUTERONOMY 11:1

∞

For if ye shall diligently keep all these commandments which I command you, to do them, to love the LORD your God, to walk in all his ways, and to cleave unto him; then will the LORD drive out all these nations from before you, and ye shall possess greater nations and mightier than yourselves.

DEUTERONOMY 11:22–23

∞

And the LORD thy God will circumcise thine heart, and the heart of thy seed, to love the LORD thy God with all thine heart, and with all thy soul, that thou mayest live.

DEUTERONOMY 30:6

I have set before you life and death, blessing and cursing: therefore choose life, that both thou and thy seed may live: that thou mayest love the LORD thy God, and that thou mayest obey his voice, and that thou mayest cleave unto him: for he is thy life, and the length of thy days.

DEUTERONOMY 30:19–20

But take diligent heed to do the commandment and the law, which Moses the servant of the LORD charged you, to love the LORD your God, and to walk in all his ways, and to keep his commandments, and to cleave unto him, and to serve him with all your heart and with all your soul.

JOSHUA 22:5

Because he hath set his love upon me, therefore will I deliver him: I will set him on high, because he hath known my name.

PSALM 91:14

Master, which is the great commandment in the law? Jesus said unto him, Thou shalt love the Lord thy God with all thy heart, and with all thy soul, and with all thy mind. This is the first and great commandment.

MATTHEW 22:36–38

If ye love me, keep my commandments.

JOHN 14:15

He that hath my commandments, and keepeth them, he it is that loveth me: and he that loveth me shall be loved of my Father, and I will love him, and will manifest myself to him.

JOHN 14:21

If ye keep my commandments, ye shall abide in my love; even as I have kept my Father's commandments, and abide in his love.

JOHN 15:10

Eye hath not seen, nor ear heard, neither have entered into the heart of man, the things which God hath prepared for them that love him.

1 CORINTHIANS 2:9

We love him, because he first loved us.

1 JOHN 4:19

If a man say, I love God, and hateth his brother, he is a liar: for he that loveth not his brother whom he hath seen, how can he love God whom he hath not seen?

1 JOHN 4:20

For this is the love of God, that we keep his commandments: and his commandments are not grievous.

1 JOHN 5:3

6. SEEKING GOD

What does it mean to *seek* God? Is He hiding? Well, odd as this may sound, the answer is yes. Isaiah pointed out, "Verily thou art a God that hidest thyself" (Isaiah 45:15). You may have noticed that 99.99 percent of the time, God can't be seen. In fact, Paul calls Him "the invisible God" (Colossians 1:15).

In the Bible, men like Moses "endured, as seeing him who is invisible" (Hebrews 11:27). They couldn't actually *see* God, but they proceeded, trusting that He was real even though He was invisible and intangible. "For we walk by faith, not by sight" (2 Corinthians 5:7). You can't see God, but you can know He's there by the way He protects you, provides for you, and does little miracles for you every day.

When people sin or neglect Him, however, God often removes *all* signs of His presence, which forces them to search for Him. Paul said that men "should seek the Lord, if haply they might. . .find him, though he be not far from every one of us" (Acts 17:27).

So often, however, people seek God only for a brief time. They don't keep at it until they actually find Him. So *keep* seeking the Lord until you know you've touched Him. And once you've found Him, abide in that secret place (Psalm 91:1).

Glory ye in his holy name: let the heart of them rejoice that seek the LORD. Seek the LORD and his strength, seek his face continually.

1 CHRONICLES 16:10–11

The LORD is with you, while ye be with him; and if ye seek him, he will be found of you; but if ye forsake him, he will forsake you.

2 CHRONICLES 15:2

And he sought God in the days of Zechariah. . .and as long as he sought the LORD, God made him to prosper.

2 CHRONICLES 26:5

One thing have I desired of the LORD, that will I seek after; that I may dwell in the house of the LORD all the days of my life, to behold the beauty of the LORD, and to enquire in his temple.

PSALM 27:4

∽

When thou saidst, Seek ye my face; my heart said unto thee, Thy face, LORD, will I seek.

PSALM 27:8

∽

O God, thou art my God; early will I seek thee: my soul thirsteth for thee, my flesh longeth for thee in a dry and thirsty land, where no water is; to see thy power and thy glory, so as I have seen thee in the sanctuary.

PSALM 63:1–2

But it is good for me to draw near to God: I have put my trust in the Lord GOD, that I may declare all thy works.

PSALM 73:28

❧

He that dwelleth in the secret place of the most High shall abide under the shadow of the Almighty. I will say of the LORD, He is my refuge and my fortress: my God; in him will I trust.

PSALM 91:1–2

❧

Because thou hast made the LORD, which is my refuge, even the most High, thy habitation; there shall no evil befall thee.

PSALM 91:9–10

❧

Seek ye the LORD while he may be found, call ye upon him while he is near.

ISAIAH 55:6

❧

And ye shall seek me, and find me, when ye shall search for me with all your heart.

JEREMIAH 29:13

❧

Call unto me, and I will answer thee, and show thee great and mighty things, which thou knowest not.

JEREMIAH 33:3

❧

The LORD is good unto them that wait for him, to the soul that seeketh him.

LAMENTATIONS 3:25

And I set my face unto the Lord God, to seek by prayer and supplications, with fasting, and sackcloth, and ashes.

DANIEL 9:3

∞

I will go and return to my place, till they acknowledge their offence, and seek my face: in their affliction they will seek me early.

HOSEA 5:15

∞

Sow to yourselves in righteousness, reap in mercy; break up your fallow ground: for it is time to seek the LORD, till he come and rain righteousness upon you.

HOSEA 10:12

∞

And he cometh unto the disciples, and findeth them asleep, and saith unto Peter, What, could ye not watch with me one hour?

MATTHEW 26:40

∞

And in the morning, rising up a great while before day, he went out, and departed into a solitary place, and there prayed.

MARK 1:35

∞

But the hour cometh, and now is, when the true worshippers shall worship the Father in spirit and in truth: for the Father seeketh such to worship him. God is a Spirit: and they that worship him must worship him in spirit and in truth.

JOHN 4:23–24

7. PRAYER PRINCIPLES

There are a number of prayer principles in the Bible. The writer of Hebrews said that "he that cometh to God must believe that he is, *and* that he is a rewarder of them that diligently seek him" (Hebrews 11:6, emphasis added).

There are two thoughts here. First, you must believe that God exists and has the power to answer prayer. There's no sense in praying if you doubt these. Second, you must believe that if you pray and don't give up, then God will eventually give what you're asking for.

You must have faith not only that God grants requests, but that He will grant *this* particular request. "What things soever ye desire, when ye pray, believe that ye receive them, and ye shall have them" (Mark 11:24).

Another prayer principle is that what you're praying for must be within God's will. "If we ask any thing according to his will, he heareth us: and if we know that he hear us, whatsoever we ask, we know that we *have* the petitions that we desired of him" (1 John 5:14–15, emphasis added).

A final prayer principle is that you must be obedient to God. "And whatsoever we ask, we receive of him, because we keep his commandments, and do those things that are pleasing in his sight" (1 John 3:22).

Because he hath set his love upon me. . .he shall call upon me, and I will answer him: I will be with him in trouble; I will deliver him, and honour him.

PSALM 91:14–15

And when thou prayest, thou shalt not be as the hypocrites are: for they love to pray standing in the synagogues and in the corners of the streets, that they may be seen of men. Verily I say unto you, They have their reward. But thou, when thou prayest, enter into thy closet, and when thou hast shut thy door, pray to thy Father which is in secret; and thy Father which seeth in secret shall reward thee openly.

MATTHEW 6:5–6

But when ye pray, use not vain repetitions, as the heathen do: for they think that they shall be heard for their much speaking. Be not ye therefore like unto them: for your Father knoweth what things ye have need of, before ye ask him.

MATTHEW 6:7–8

After this manner therefore pray ye: Our Father which art in heaven, Hallowed be thy name. Thy kingdom come, Thy will be done in earth, as it is in heaven. Give us this day our daily bread. And forgive us our debts, as we forgive our debtors. And lead us not into temptation, but deliver us from evil: For thine is the kingdom, and the power, and the glory, for ever. Amen.

MATTHEW 6:9–13

Ask, and it shall be given you; seek, and ye shall find; knock, and it shall be opened unto you: for every one that asketh receiveth; and he that seeketh findeth; and to him that knocketh it shall be opened.

MATTHEW 7:7–8

❧

And all things, whatsoever ye shall ask in prayer, believing, ye shall receive.

MATTHEW 21:22

❧

Therefore I say unto you, What things soever ye desire, when ye pray, believe that ye receive them, and ye shall have them.

MARK 11:24

❧

And when ye stand praying, forgive, if ye have ought against any: that your Father also which is in heaven may forgive you your trespasses.

MARK 11:25

❧

And he spake a parable unto them to this end, that men ought always to pray, and not to faint.

LUKE 18:1

❧

Now we know that God heareth not sinners: but if any man be a worshipper of God, and doeth his will, him he heareth.

JOHN 9:31

And whatsoever ye shall ask in my name, that will I do, that the Father may be glorified in the Son. If ye shall ask any thing in my name, I will do it.

JOHN 14:13–14

∽

Verily, verily, I say unto you, Whatsoever ye shall ask the Father in my name, he will give it you.

JOHN 16:23

∽

Be careful for nothing; but in every thing by prayer and supplication with thanksgiving let your requests be made known unto God.

PHILIPPIANS 4:6

∽

Ye have not, because ye ask not.

JAMES 4:2

∽

And whatsoever we ask, we receive of him, because we keep his commandments, and do those things that are pleasing in his sight.

I JOHN 3:22

∽

And this is the confidence that we have in him, that, if we ask any thing according to his will, he heareth us: and if we know that he hear us, whatsoever we ask, we know that we have the petitions that we desired of him.

I JOHN 5:14–15

8. PRAISE AND WORSHIP

Why are you told to praise and worship God? You might wonder if a deity who enjoys listening to repeated praise has an ego problem. This isn't the case. God commands you to praise Him for His power, His love, and His mercy because you desperately need to grasp just how magnificent He is. Most people go through life with such a limited understanding of God. But worship brings you into a greater revelation of your heavenly Father.

The more powerful and loving and merciful you understand God to be, the more you're able to trust that He's able and willing to bless you—and your faith then enables Him to pour out His love and blessing into your life.

All the wonderful things that men and women in the Bible wrote when praising God weren't exaggerations. They were true. They were fact. You're asked to simply "give unto the LORD the glory *due* unto his name" (1 Chronicles 16:29, emphasis added).

Truth be told, you benefit from worshipping God far more than He does. Psalm 22:3 declares, "But thou art holy, O thou that inhabitest the praises of Israel." God is present in a very real way when you praise Him. You open the door for His presence and power to bless, to inspire, to strengthen, and to heal you. So praise Him today.

*And I bowed down my head, and worshipped the LORD,
and blessed the LORD God.*

GENESIS 24:48

∞

*And it came to pass, that, when Abraham's servant heard
their words, he worshipped the LORD, bowing himself to
the earth.*

GENESIS 24:52

∞

*I will call on the LORD, who is worthy to be praised:
so shall I be saved from mine enemies.*

2 SAMUEL 22:4

∞

*Give unto the LORD the glory due unto his name: bring an
offering, and come before him: worship the LORD in the
beauty of holiness.*

1 CHRONICLES 16:29

∞

*And when all the children of Israel saw how the fire came
down, and the glory of the LORD upon the house, they
bowed themselves with their faces to the ground upon the
pavement, and worshipped, and praised the LORD, saying,
For he is good; for his mercy endureth for ever.*

2 CHRONICLES 7:3

∞

*And Ezra blessed the LORD, the great God. And all the
people answered, Amen, Amen, with lifting up their
hands: and they bowed their heads, and worshipped the
LORD with their faces to the ground.*

NEHEMIAH 8:6

But as for me, I will come into thy house in the multitude
of thy mercy: and in thy fear will I worship toward thy
holy temple.

PSALM 5:7

∞

I will praise thee, O LORD, with my whole heart; I will
shew forth all thy marvellous works.

PSALM 9:1

∞

Rejoice in the LORD, O ye righteous: for praise is comely for
the upright.

PSALM 33:1

∞

I will bless the LORD at all times: his praise shall
continually be in my mouth.

PSALM 34:1

∞

I will freely sacrifice unto thee: I will praise thy name,
O LORD; for it is good.

PSALM 54:6

∞

Because thy lovingkindness is better than life, my lips shall
praise thee.

PSALM 63:3

∞

I will praise thee, O Lord my God, with all my heart:
and I will glorify thy name for evermore.

PSALM 86:12

It is a good thing to give thanks unto the LORD, and to sing praises unto thy name, O Most High.

PSALM 92:1

∞

O come, let us worship and bow down: let us kneel before the LORD our maker.

PSALM 95:6

∞

Exalt ye the LORD our God, and worship at his footstool; for he is holy.

PSALM 99:5

∞

Oh that men would praise the LORD for his goodness, and for his wonderful works to the children of men!

PSALM 107:8

∞

Praise ye the LORD. I will praise the LORD with my whole heart.

PSALM 111:1

∞

Praise ye the LORD. Praise ye the name of the LORD; praise him, O ye servants of the LORD.

PSALM 135:1

∞

While I live will I praise the LORD: I will sing praises unto my God while I have any being.

PSALM 146:2

9. READING GOD'S WORD

Many Christians hardly ever read their Bibles. They know there are "good principles" in the Sermon on the Mount, and are aware that reading Psalm 23 can comfort them when they're troubled, but other than that, they don't often read the Bible. They think it's a boring book full of endless begats, ancient history, and religious rules no longer relevant today.

But God's Word is anything but dead and irrelevant. Moses wrote of God's Law in the Old Testament, "It is not a vain thing for you; because it is your life" (Deuteronomy 32:47). And Jesus said regarding His teachings in the New Testament, "The words that I speak unto you, they are spirit, and they are life" (John 6:63).

True, you find eternal life through a personal encounter with Jesus Christ. You don't find it by simply reading a Bible. But daily reading and meditating on God's Word gives you power and inspiration and a closeness to God that is essential in this hectic day and age.

Jeremiah said, "Thy words were found, and I did eat them; and thy word was unto me the joy and rejoicing of mine heart" (Jeremiah 15:16). Just as you must chew, swallow, and digest physical food for it to do your body any good, even so you must devour the heavenly manna, the Word of God.

And these words, which I command thee this day, shall be in thine heart: and thou shalt. . .talk of them when thou sittest in thine house, and when thou walkest by the way, and when thou liest down, and when thou risest up.

DEUTERONOMY 6:6–7

∞

And he humbled thee, and suffered thee to hunger, and fed thee with manna, which thou knewest not, neither did thy fathers know; that he might make thee know that man doth not live by bread only, but by every word that proceedeth out of the mouth of the LORD doth man live.

DEUTERONOMY 8:3

∞

Therefore shall ye lay up these my words in your heart and in your soul.

DEUTERONOMY 11:18

∞

Set your hearts unto all the words which I testify among you this day, which ye shall command your children to observe to do, all the words of this law. For it is not a vain thing for you; because it is your life.

DEUTERONOMY 32:46–47

∞

When ye received the word of God which ye heard of us, ye received it not as the word of men, but as it is in truth, the word of God, which effectually worketh also in you that believe.

1 THESSALONIANS 2:13

*And all the people gathered themselves together as one man
into the street that was before the water gate; and they
spake unto Ezra the scribe to bring the book of the law of
Moses, which the LORD had commanded to Israel. And
Ezra the priest brought the law before the congregation
both of men and women, and all that could hear with understanding, upon the first day of the seventh month. And
he read therein. . .from the morning until midday, before
the men and the women, and those that could understand;
and the ears of all the people were attentive unto the book
of the law.*

NEHEMIAH 8:1–3

∞

*Neither have I gone back from the commandment of his
lips; I have esteemed the words of his mouth more than my
necessary food.*

JOB 23:12

∞

*Thy word have I hid in mine heart, that I might not sin
against thee.*

PSALM 119:11

∞

*Open thou mine eyes, that I may behold wondrous things
out of thy law.*

PSALM 119:18

∞

Thy word is a lamp unto my feet, and a light unto my path.

PSALM 119:105

Thy words were found, and I did eat them; and thy word was unto me the joy and rejoicing of mine heart: for I am called by thy name, O LORD God of hosts.

JEREMIAH 15:16

∞

It is the spirit that quickeneth; the flesh profiteth nothing: the words that I speak unto you, they are spirit, and they are life.

JOHN 6:63

∞

If ye continue in my word, then are ye my disciples indeed; and ye shall know the truth, and the truth shall make you free.

JOHN 8:31–32

∞

When they had gathered the multitude together, they delivered the epistle: which when they had read, they rejoiced for the consolation.

ACTS 15:30–31

∞

Till I come, give attendance to reading, to exhortation, to doctrine.

1 TIMOTHY 4:13

∞

All scripture is given by inspiration of God, and is profitable for doctrine, for reproof, for correction, for instruction in righteousness.

2 TIMOTHY 3:16

10. UNDERSTANDING GOD'S WAYS

Can you understand God? Many people quote Isaiah 55:9, which says, "For as the heavens are higher than the earth, so are my ways higher than your ways, and my thoughts than your thoughts"—and give up trying to understand Him at all.

But remember, part of the greatest commandment is to "love the Lord thy God. . .with all thy *mind*" (Matthew 22:37, emphasis added). Like countless men and women down through the ages, you are to seek His wisdom. "It is the glory of God to conceal a thing: but the honour of kings is to search out a matter" (Proverbs 25:2). And as you walk close to Him daily, you increase in wisdom, and you *do* understand more about God's ways.

But this understanding can only go so far. Many situations are well beyond your skill set. Then it's wise to simply trust God even though you can't understand what He's doing—just as you trust experts to design a nuclear power plant, and other experts to run it.

If you're in a season when things seem under control, you can get the idea that life and God are pretty simple. But face a financial setback or suffer poor health or relationship problems, and you're immediately in over your head, the world becomes complex and incomprehensible, and you need to put your hand into God's and trust Him.

By his spirit he hath garnished the heavens; his hand hath formed the crooked serpent. Lo, these are parts of his ways: but how little a portion is heard of him? but the thunder of his power who can understand?

JOB 26:13–14

∞

Whence then cometh wisdom? and where is the place of understanding? Seeing it is hid from the eyes of all living. . . . God understandeth the way thereof, and he knoweth the place thereof. For he looketh to the ends of the earth, and seeth under the whole heaven.

JOB 28:20–21, 23–24

∞

Commit thy way unto the LORD; trust also in him; and he shall bring it to pass.

PSALM 37:5

∞

Give me understanding, and I shall keep thy law; yea, I shall observe it with my whole heart.

PSALM 119:34

∞

Great is our Lord, and of great power: his understanding is infinite.

PSALM 147:5

∞

Yea, if thou criest after knowledge, and liftest up thy voice for understanding; if thou seekest her as silver, and searchest for her as for hid treasures; then shalt thou understand the fear of the LORD, and find the knowledge of God.

PROVERBS 2:3–5

Trust in the LORD *with all thine heart; and lean not unto thine own understanding. In all thy ways acknowledge him, and he shall direct thy paths.*

PROVERBS 3:5–6

∞

There is a way that seemeth right unto a man, but the end thereof are the ways of death.

PROVERBS 16:25

∞

Man's goings are of the LORD; *how can a man then understand his own way?*

PROVERBS 20:24

∞

It is the glory of God to conceal a thing: but the honour of kings is to search out a matter.

PROVERBS 25:2

∞

Who hath measured the waters in the hollow of his hand, and meted out heaven with the span, and comprehended the dust of the earth in a measure, and weighed the mountains in scales, and the hills in a balance? Who hath directed the Spirit of the LORD, *or being his counsellor hath taught him? With whom took he counsel, and who instructed him, and taught him in the path of judgment, and taught him knowledge, and shewed to him the way of understanding?*

ISAIAH 40:12–14

For who hath known the mind of the Lord, that he may instruct him? but we have the mind of Christ.

1 CORINTHIANS 2:16

∞

And I will bring the blind by a way that they knew not; I will lead them in paths that they have not known: I will make darkness light before them, and crooked things straight.

ISAIAH 42:16

∞

For my thoughts are not your thoughts, neither are your ways my ways, saith the LORD. For as the heavens are higher than the earth, so are my ways higher than your ways, and my thoughts than your thoughts.

ISAIAH 55:8–9

∞

Who is wise, and he shall understand these things? prudent, and he shall know them? for the ways of the LORD are right, and the just shall walk in them: but the transgressors shall fall therein.

HOSEA 14:9

∞

Now when they had gone throughout Phrygia and the region of Galatia, and were forbidden of the Holy Ghost to preach the word in Asia, after they were come to Mysia, they assayed to go into Bithynia: but the Spirit suffered them not.

ACTS 16:6–7

11. SEEKING GOD'S WILL

You're eager to please someone you love. So if you obey the greatest commandment and "love the LORD thy God with all thine heart" (Deuteronomy 6:5), you'll be more inclined to say, "I delight to do thy will, O my God" (Psalm 40:8).

God has made much of His will plain in His Word, so if you study and attempt to live what His Word says, you'll be taking care of the biggest part of His will.

Of course, you'll still need to give prayer and thought to things, to determine what God's plans are for your life in other areas. For example, when deciding on a career or making a major business decision, you'll have to diligently seek God's face and find out what He wants you to do.

Some people think God has planned every single detail of their life, so they even pray for His perfect will when reading through a dinner menu. But if you love the Lord and want to obey Him, He often gives you a choice of different good and acceptable options—even when it comes to choosing a husband or wife. Paul said a woman "is at liberty to be married to whom she will; only in the Lord" (1 Corinthians 7:39). She can marry any man she chooses, and God has only one stipulation—that he be a believer.

So they read in the book in the law of God distinctly, and gave the sense, and caused them to understand the reading.

NEHEMIAH 8:8

∞

I delight to do thy will, O my God: yea, thy law is within my heart.

PSALM 40:8

∞

Teach me to do thy will; for thou art my God: thy spirit is good; lead me into the land of uprightness.

PSALM 143:10

∞

Trust in the LORD with all thine heart; and lean not unto thine own understanding. In all thy ways acknowledge him, and he shall direct thy paths.

PROVERBS 3:5–6

∞

That the living may know that the most High ruleth in the kingdom of men, and giveth it to whomsoever he will, and setteth up over it the basest of men.

DANIEL 4:17

∞

And all the inhabitants of the earth are reputed as nothing: and he doeth according to his will in the army of heaven, and among the inhabitants of the earth: and none can stay his hand, or say unto him, What doest thou?

DANIEL 4:35

Then shall we know, if we follow on to know the LORD.

HOSEA 6:3

∽

Thy kingdom come, Thy will be done in earth, as it is in heaven.

MATTHEW 6:10

∽

Not every one that saith unto me, Lord, Lord, shall enter into the kingdom of heaven; but he that doeth the will of my Father which is in heaven.

MATTHEW 7:21

∽

Father, if thou be willing, remove this cup from me: nevertheless not my will, but thine, be done.

LUKE 22:42

∽

Jesus saith unto them, My meat is to do the will of him that sent me, and to finish his work.

JOHN 4:34

∽

I can of mine own self do nothing: as I hear, I judge: and my judgment is just; because I seek not mine own will, but the will of the Father which hath sent me.

JOHN 5:30

∽

For I came down from heaven, not to do mine own will, but the will of him that sent me.

JOHN 6:38

If any man will do his will, he shall know of the doctrine,
whether it be of God, or whether I speak of myself.

JOHN 7:17

∞

Behold, thou art called a Jew, and restest in the law, and
makest thy boast of God, and knowest his will, and
approvest the things that are more excellent, being
instructed out of the law.

ROMANS 2:17–18

∞

In whom also we have obtained an inheritance, being
predestinated according to the purpose of him who worketh
all things after the counsel of his own will.

EPHESIANS 1:11

∞

Not with eyeservice, as menpleasers; but as the servants of
Christ, doing the will of God from the heart.

EPHESIANS 6:6

∞

For this cause we also, since the day we heard it, do not
cease to pray for you, and to desire that ye might be filled
with the knowledge of his will in all wisdom and spiritual
understanding.

COLOSSIANS 1:9

∞

And the world passeth away, and the lust thereof: but he
that doeth the will of God abideth for ever.

1 JOHN 2:17

12. SUBMITTING TO GOD

God gave the Israelites many commandments in the Law and promised that if they would not only *meditate* on them but also "*do* according to all that is written," then they would "have good success" (Joshua 1:8, emphasis added).

Where this gets really relevant is when Moses said that God would raise up another Prophet—Jesus the Messiah—who would speak God's words, and that God's people were to obey Him (Deuteronomy 18:18–19; Acts 3:22). It's wonderful to feel emotions of love for Jesus, but remember that He said, "If ye love me, keep my commandments" (John 14:15). He also said, "He that hath my commandments, and keepeth them, he it is that loveth me" (John 14:21).

However, God's people don't always readily obey Him. The Israelites often disobeyed Moses, and Christians often disobey Jesus. His command to love others, even your enemies, can be very difficult to obey. That's where the process of *submitting* to God comes in. You must make a conscious, deliberate effort to focus on His commands, seek to understand them, desire their benefits, and follow what they say.

James instructed Christians, "Submit yourselves. . . to God" (James 4:7). *Submission* is defined as "the action of accepting or yielding to the will or authority of another person." It often is not an instant action but takes time—a lifetime, in fact.

Ye shall observe to do therefore as the LORD your God hath commanded you: ye shall not turn aside to the right hand or to the left.

DEUTERONOMY 5:32

∞

For if ye shall diligently keep all these commandments which I command you, to do them, to love the LORD your God, to walk in all his ways, and to cleave unto him; then will the LORD drive out all these nations from before you, and ye shall possess greater nations and mightier than yourselves.

DEUTERONOMY 11:22–23

∞

Ye shall walk after the LORD your God, and fear him, and keep his commandments, and obey his voice, and ye shall serve him, and cleave unto him.

DEUTERONOMY 13:4

∞

This day the LORD thy God hath commanded thee to do these statutes and judgments: thou shalt therefore keep and do them with all thine heart, and with all thy soul.

DEUTERONOMY 26:16

∞

Take heed, and hearken, O Israel; this day thou art become the people of the LORD thy God. Thou shalt therefore obey the voice of the LORD thy God, and do his commandments and his statutes, which I command thee this day.

DEUTERONOMY 27:9–10

*This book of the law shall not depart out of thy mouth;
but thou shalt meditate therein day and night, that thou
mayest observe to do according to all that is written
therein: for then thou shalt make thy way prosperous,
and then thou shalt have good success.*

JOSHUA 1:8

*And he did that which was right in the sight of the LORD,
and walked in all the way of David his father, and turned
not aside to the right hand or to the left.*

2 KINGS 22:2

*The haters of the LORD should have submitted themselves
unto him: but their time should have endured for ever.*

PSALM 81:15

*Give me understanding, and I shall keep thy law; yea,
I shall observe it with my whole heart.*

PSALM 119:34

*Let us hear the conclusion of the whole matter: Fear God, and
keep his commandments: for this is the whole duty of man.*

ECCLESIASTES 12:13

*If ye be willing and obedient, ye shall eat the good of the
land.*

ISAIAH 1:19

He hath shewed thee, O man, what is good; and what doth the LORD require of thee, but to do justly, and to love mercy, and to walk humbly with thy God?

MICAH 6:8

∞

If ye know these things, happy are ye if ye do them.

JOHN 13:17

∞

If ye love me, keep my commandments.

JOHN 14:15

∞

He that hath my commandments, and keepeth them, he it is that loveth me: and he that loveth me shall be loved of my Father, and I will love him, and will manifest myself to him.

JOHN 14:21

∞

For they being ignorant of God's righteousness, and going about to establish their own righteousness, have not submitted themselves unto the righteousness of God.

ROMANS 10:3

∞

I beseech you therefore, brethren, by the mercies of God, that ye present your bodies a living sacrifice, holy, acceptable unto God, which is your reasonable service.

ROMANS 12:1

13. TRUSTING GOD

It's human nature to be concerned when things aren't working out, because you know that if things *don't* come through for you, you'll suffer hardship or lack. But having done your best to resolve an issue, you then have a choice: either you can commit it to God and trust Him to do what you can't do; or you can *continue* to try to solve it with your own wisdom and energy, and worry about it.

Say your computer isn't working. You've done everything you can think of, but the problem is definitely beyond you. So you take it to a technician. If you trust him, you leave it in his hands and check in with him later. If you get impatient and fret, however, you may grab your computer back and continue tinkering with it. It's like that with God.

You often must make a daily, ongoing decision to trust God instead of worrying. But it can be difficult to trust. The problem is often that His solution doesn't make sense to you. You don't understand His logic.

But that's the whole point: If God were operating according to *your* level of understanding, He'd be stuck where you are. But because He's God, He takes a completely different approach to things. So trust that He knows what He's doing.

And she said, As the LORD thy God liveth, I have not a cake, but an handful of meal in a barrel, and a little oil in a cruse: and, behold, I am gathering two sticks, that I may go in and dress it for me and my son, that we may eat it, and die. And Elijah said unto her, Fear not; go and do as thou hast said: but make me thereof a little cake first, and bring it unto me, and after make for thee and for thy son. For thus saith the LORD God of Israel, The barrel of meal shall not waste, neither shall the cruse of oil fail, until the day that the LORD sendeth rain upon the earth. And she went and did according to the saying of Elijah: and she, and he, and her house, did eat many days.

1 KINGS 17:12–15

He trusted in the LORD God of Israel; so that after him was none like him among all the kings of Judah, nor any that were before him.

2 KINGS 18:5

O LORD my God, in thee do I put my trust: save me from all them that persecute me, and deliver me.

PSALM 7:1

And they that know thy name will put their trust in thee: for thou, LORD, hast not forsaken them that seek thee.

PSALM 9:10

The LORD is my rock, and my fortress, and my deliverer; my God, my strength, in whom I will trust.

PSALM 18:2

The Lord is my strength and my shield; my heart trusted in him, and I am helped: therefore my heart greatly rejoiceth; and with my song will I praise him.

Psalm 28:7

∞

O taste and see that the Lord is good: blessed is the man that trusteth in him.

Psalm 34:8

∞

Take no thought for your life, what ye shall eat, or what ye shall drink; nor yet for your body, what ye shall put on. Is not the life more than meat, and the body than raiment? Behold the fowls of the air: for they sow not, neither do they reap, nor gather into barns; yet your heavenly Father feedeth them. Are ye not much better than they? Which of you by taking thought can add one cubit unto his stature? And why take ye thought for raiment? Consider the lilies of the field, how they grow; they toil not, neither do they spin: And yet I say unto you, That even Solomon in all his glory was not arrayed like one of these. Wherefore, if God so clothe the grass of the field, which to day is, and to morrow is cast into the oven, shall he not much more clothe you, O ye of little faith? Therefore take no thought, saying, What shall we eat? or, What shall we drink? or, Wherewithal shall we be clothed? . . . For your heavenly Father knoweth that ye have need of all these things. But seek ye first the kingdom of God, and his righteousness; and all these things shall be added unto you. Take therefore no thought for the morrow: for the morrow shall take thought for the things of itself.

Matthew 6:25–34

Be careful for nothing; but in every thing by prayer and supplication with thanksgiving let your requests be made known unto God.

PHILIPPIANS 4:6

Casting all your care upon him; for he careth for you.

1 PETER 5:7

14. FAITH AND BELIEVING

In the Gospels, Jesus often chided His disciples for their weak faith. He said to them, "O ye of little faith" or "O thou of little faith" *five* times. For their part, "the apostles said unto the Lord, Increase our faith" (Luke 17:5). That is a wise response. And how does God normally increase your faith? Faith usually comes from faithfully reading the Word of God (Romans 10:17).

Great faith, the kind of faith that moves mountains, is a gift of the Spirit (1 Corinthians 12:9). Whether or not you have this kind of faith has very little to do with any merit you may have. Rather, God gives His gifts of the Spirit—including the gift of great faith—according to His sovereign will (1 Corinthians 12:7, 9, 11).

But you *do* have a part to play in steadily increasing the kind of faith you need in facing day-to-day situations. Though it might come as a surprise to hear this, you can actually *choose* to have faith or not to have faith.

In Jesus' day, many Jews in Jerusalem, seeing His miracles, believed on Him; but many *refused* to be convinced, no matter how many miracles He did (John 11:45; 12:37). They had made up their minds not to believe. So make up your mind to believe, so that God can bless you.

But when he saw the wind boisterous, he was afraid; and beginning to sink, he cried, saying, Lord, save me. And immediately Jesus stretched forth his hand, and caught him, and said unto him, O thou of little faith, wherefore didst thou doubt?

MATTHEW 14:30–31

⚬

Verily I say unto you, If ye have faith, and doubt not, ye shall not only do this which is done to the fig tree, but also if ye shall say unto this mountain, Be thou removed, and be thou cast into the sea; it shall be done. And all things, whatsoever ye shall ask in prayer, believing, ye shall receive.

MATTHEW 21:21–22

⚬

And he could there do no mighty work, save that he laid his hands upon a few sick folk, and healed them. And he marvelled because of their unbelief.

MARK 6:5–6

⚬

And ofttimes it hath cast him into the fire, and into the waters, to destroy him: but if thou canst do any thing, have compassion on us, and help us. Jesus said unto him, If thou canst believe, all things are possible to him that believeth. And straightway the father of the child cried out, and said with tears, Lord, I believe; help thou mine unbelief.

MARK 9:22–24

⚬

And Jesus answering saith unto them, Have faith in God.

MARK 11:22

Verily, verily, I say unto you, He that believeth on me, the works that I do shall he do also; and greater works than these shall he do.

JOHN 14:12

∞

And being not weak in faith, he considered not his own body now dead, when he was about an hundred years old, neither yet the deadness of Sarah's womb: he staggered not at the promise of God through unbelief; but was strong in faith, giving glory to God; and being fully persuaded that, what he had promised, he was able also to perform.

ROMANS 4:19–21

∞

While we look not at the things which are seen, but at the things which are not seen: for the things which are seen are temporal; but the things which are not seen are eternal.

2 CORINTHIANS 4:18

∞

For we walk by faith, not by sight.

2 CORINTHIANS 5:7

∞

Now unto him that is able to do exceeding abundantly above all that we ask or think, according to the power that worketh in us, unto him be glory.

EPHESIANS 3:20–21

∞

Now the just shall live by faith.

HEBREWS 10:38

By faith he forsook Egypt, not fearing the wrath of the king: for he endured, as seeing him who is invisible.

HEBREWS 11:27

❧

Now faith is the substance of things hoped for, the evidence of things not seen.

HEBREWS 11:1

❧

But without faith it is impossible to please him: for he that cometh to God must believe that he is, and that he is a rewarder of them that diligently seek him.

HEBREWS 11:6

❧

But let him ask in faith, nothing wavering. For he that wavereth is like a wave of the sea driven with the wind and tossed. For let not that man think that he shall receive any thing of the Lord. A double minded man is unstable in all his ways.

JAMES 1:6–8

❧

For whatsoever is born of God overcometh the world: and this is the victory that overcometh the world, even our faith.

1 JOHN 5:4

15. VICTORY OVER THE DEVIL

Jesus Christ, the Son of God, has total victory over the devil and all his demons, and because Jesus lives in your heart, you too can have victory. You "have overcome them: because greater is he that is in you, than he that is in the world" (1 John 4:4).

However, you need to keep your heart right with God if you wish to have continual protection from the devil. This is why Paul cautions, "Neither give place to the devil" (Ephesians 4:27). You give the enemy of your soul place to work when you willfully disobey God. Sin creates a breach in your spiritual defenses and allows Satan to take advantage of you and attack you (2 Corinthians 2:11). So repent today.

One sure way to continually have victory over the enemy is to soak yourself in God's Word. It pays not only to read the Bible but to memorize key promises and quote them during times of testing. As the apostle John said, "The word of God abideth in you, and ye have overcome the wicked one" (1 John 2:14).

A good promise to memorize is James 4:7, which says, "Resist the devil, and he will flee from you." It may take sustained resistance for a time, but if you stand in the power of God's Spirit, the devil *has* to flee.

But if I cast out devils by the Spirit of God, then the kingdom of God is come unto you.

MATTHEW 12:28

∞

And these signs shall follow them that believe; In my name shall they cast out devils.

MARK 16:17

∞

And they were all amazed, and spake among themselves, saying, What a word is this! for with authority and power he commandeth the unclean spirits, and they come out.

LUKE 4:36

∞

And the seventy returned again with joy, saying, Lord, even the devils are subject unto us through thy name. And he said unto them, I beheld Satan as lightning fall from heaven. Behold, I give unto you power to tread on serpents and scorpions, and over all the power of the enemy: and nothing shall by any means hurt you. Notwithstanding in this rejoice not, that the spirits are subject unto you; but rather rejoice, because your names are written in heaven.

LUKE 10:17–20

∞

Now is the judgment of this world: now shall the prince of this world be cast out.

JOHN 12:31

∞

And the God of peace shall bruise Satan under your feet shortly.

ROMANS 16:20

But if our gospel be hid, it is hid to them that are lost: in whom the god of this world hath blinded the minds of them which believe not, lest the light of the glorious gospel of Christ, who is the image of God, should shine unto them.

2 CORINTHIANS 4:3–4

∞

Wherein in time past ye walked according to the course of this world, according to the prince of the power of the air, the spirit that now worketh in the children of disobedience.

EPHESIANS 2:2

∞

Neither give place to the devil.

EPHESIANS 4:27

∞

Put on the whole armour of God, that ye may be able to stand against the wiles of the devil. For we wrestle not against flesh and blood, but against principalities, against powers, against the rulers of the darkness of this world, against spiritual wickedness in high places.

EPHESIANS 6:11–12

∞

Above all, taking the shield of faith, wherewith ye shall be able to quench all the fiery darts of the wicked.

EPHESIANS 6:16

∞

And having spoiled principalities and powers, he made a shew of them openly, triumphing over them in it.

COLOSSIANS 2:15

Thou believest that there is one God; thou doest well: the devils also believe, and tremble.

JAMES 2:19

∞

Forasmuch then as the children are partakers of flesh and blood, he also himself likewise took part of the same; that through death he might destroy him that had the power of death, that is, the devil.

HEBREWS 2:14

∞

Submit yourselves therefore to God. Resist the devil, and he will flee from you.

JAMES 4:7

∞

Be sober, be vigilant; because your adversary the devil, as a roaring lion, walketh about, seeking whom he may devour: whom resist stedfast in the faith.

1 PETER 5:8–9

∞

I have written unto you, young men, because ye are strong, and the word of God abideth in you, and ye have overcome the wicked one.

1 JOHN 2:14

∞

He that committeth sin is of the devil; for the devil sinneth from the beginning. For this purpose the Son of God was manifested, that he might destroy the works of the devil.

1 JOHN 3:8

16. PERSISTENCE

Some people are naturally persistent. They don't take no for an answer. When they want something, they keep insisting that someone give it to them. Or they keep demanding that someone do something for them. They want what they want—and they often get it.

If you're like *most* people, however, you tend to give up after a while. So Jesus encouraged His disciples to persist and not give up. This applies whether you're standing up for your rights or trying to follow the Lord. You're even to be persistent with God! In the parable of the three loaves (Luke 11:5–9) and the parable of the persistent widow (Luke 18:1–5), Jesus told His disciples to stay doggedly determined in prayer.

The Bible repeatedly tells you to "continue" doing something good. In other words, you're doing the right thing, so keep at it. Stick to it. Don't give up. Hold on to your faith and don't let go.

It does no good to run a long-endurance race, cover most of the distance, but then stop short of the finish line. It's the same with your walk with the Lord. Jesus said, "He that shall endure unto the end, the same shall be saved" (Matthew 24:13). Don't be like those who "endure but for a time" (Mark 4:17). Hang in there!

And, behold, two blind men sitting by the way side,
when they heard that Jesus passed by, cried out, saying,
Have mercy on us, O Lord, thou son of David. And the
multitude rebuked them, because they should hold their
peace: but they cried the more, saying, Have mercy on us,
O Lord, thou son of David.

MATTHEW 20:30–31

❧

And it came to pass in those days, that he went out into a
mountain to pray, and continued all night in prayer to God.

LUKE 6:12

❧

And he said unto them, Which of you shall have a friend,
and shall go unto him at midnight, and say unto him,
Friend, lend me three loaves; for a friend of mine in his
journey is come to me, and I have nothing to set before
him? And he from within shall answer and say, Trouble
me not: the door is now shut, and my children are with me
in bed; I cannot rise and give thee. I say unto you, Though
he will not rise and give him, because he is his friend, yet
because of his importunity he will rise and give him as
many as he needeth. And I say unto you, Ask, and it shall
be given you; seek, and ye shall find; knock, and it shall be
opened unto you.

LUKE 11:5–9

❧

Continue in prayer, and watch in the same with
thanksgiving.

COLOSSIANS 4:2

*Cast not away therefore your confidence, which hath great
recompence of reward. For ye have need of patience, that, after
ye have done the will of God, ye might receive the promise.*

HEBREWS 10:35–36

∽

*And he spake a parable unto them to this end, that men
ought always to pray, and not to faint; saying, There was
in a city a judge, which feared not God, neither regarded
man: and there was a widow in that city; and she came
unto him, saying, Avenge me of mine adversary. And
he would not for a while: but afterward he said within
himself, Though I fear not God, nor regard man; yet because
this widow troubleth me, I will avenge her, lest by her
continual coming she weary me.*

LUKE 18:1–5

∽

*Then said Jesus to those Jews which believed on him, If ye
continue in my word, then are ye my disciples indeed.*

JOHN 8:31

∽

*And they continued stedfastly in the apostles' doctrine and
fellowship, and in breaking of bread, and in prayers.*

ACTS 2:42

∽

*Many of the Jews and religious proselytes followed Paul
and Barnabas: who, speaking to them, persuaded them to
continue in the grace of God.*

ACTS 13:43

*Confirming the souls of the disciples, and exhorting them
to continue in the faith, and that we must through much
tribulation enter into the kingdom of God.*

ACTS 14:22

∞

*Praying always with all prayer and supplication in the
Spirit, and watching thereunto with all perseverance and
supplication for all saints.*

EPHESIANS 6:18

∞

*Take heed unto thyself, and unto the doctrine; continue in
them: for in doing this thou shalt both save thyself, and
them that hear thee.*

1 TIMOTHY 4:16

∞

*But continue thou in the things which thou hast learned
and hast been assured of, knowing of whom thou hast
learned them.*

2 TIMOTHY 3:14

∞

*But whoso looketh into the perfect law of liberty, and
continueth therein, he being not a forgetful hearer, but a
doer of the work, this man shall be blessed in his deed.*

JAMES 1:25

17. CHARACTER AND SELF-CONTROL

The Bible describes self-control as "ruling your own spirit" (see Proverbs 16:32). It's listed as one of the nine fruits of the Spirit, but many people aren't aware that "temperance" means "self-control." They have the idea that they can't do anything, but have to depend on God to do everything. So if they have a nicotine habit or an alcohol addiction, they don't try to control it. They wait for God to do a miracle.

While it's true that "without [Him] ye can do nothing" (John 15:5), God usually partners with you to accomplish things. Paul wrote, "I can do all things through Christ which strengtheneth me" (Philippians 4:13). Paul was the one doing "all things," but God was empowering him to do them.

God expects you to put forth some effort to cultivate virtues and to refrain from giving yourself over to vices. Paul wrote that Christians must be "not given to wine. . .not given to filthy lucre," and so on.

You must do the part you *can* do. When Jesus was about to raise Lazarus from the dead, He told the people, "Take *ye* away the stone" (John 11:39, emphasis added). Jesus didn't roll away the stone. He let the people do that. Then, when they had done what they could do, He did what they couldn't do. So don't shy away from exercising self-control.

And now, my daughter, fear not; I will do to thee all that thou requirest: for all the city of my people doth know that thou art a virtuous woman.

RUTH 3:11

And who is so faithful among all thy servants as David, which is the king's son in law, and goeth at thy bidding, and is honourable in thine house?

1 SAMUEL 22:14

And he did that which was right in the sight of the LORD, and walked in all the way of David his father, and turned not aside to the right hand or to the left.

2 KINGS 22:2

Thus David the son of Jesse reigned over all Israel. . . . And he died in a good old age, full of days, riches, and honour.

1 CHRONICLES 29:26, 28

He that is slow to anger is better than the mighty; and he that ruleth his spirit than he that taketh a city.

PROVERBS 16:32

A good name is rather to be chosen than great riches, and loving favour rather than silver and gold.

PROVERBS 22:1

And put a knife to thy throat, if thou be a man given to appetite.

PROVERBS 23:2

A man's pride shall bring him low: but honour shall uphold the humble in spirit.

PROVERBS 29:23

Who can find a virtuous woman? for her price is far above rubies. The heart of her husband doth safely trust in her, so that he shall have no need of spoil. She will do him good and not evil all the days of her life.

PROVERBS 31:10–12

A good name is better than precious ointment.

ECCLESIASTES 7:1

Dead flies cause the ointment of the apothecary to send forth a stinking savour: so doth a little folly him that is in reputation for wisdom and honour.

ECCLESIASTES 10:1

He that hath no rule over his own spirit is like a city that is broken down, and without walls.

PROVERBS 25:28

And as he reasoned of righteousness, temperance [self-control], and judgment to come, Felix trembled.

ACTS 24:25

And the spirits of the prophets are subject to the prophets.

1 CORINTHIANS 14:32

∞

But the fruit of the Spirit is love, joy, peace, longsuffering, gentleness, goodness, faith, meekness, temperance [self-control]: against such there is no law.

GALATIANS 5:22–23

∞

Not given to wine, no striker, not greedy of filthy lucre; but patient, not a brawler, not covetous.

1 TIMOTHY 3:3

∞

Likewise must the deacons be grave, not doubletongued, not given to much wine, not greedy of filthy lucre.

1 TIMOTHY 3:8

∞

For a bishop must be blameless, as the steward of God; not selfwilled, not soon angry, not given to wine, no striker, not given to filthy lucre.

TITUS 1:7

∞

The aged women likewise, that they be in behaviour as becometh holiness, not false accusers, not given to much wine, teachers of good things.

TITUS 2:3

18. DISCIPLINE AND CHASTISEMENT

When you disobey God, He disciplines you to bring you back in line. It may take you awhile to clue in to what's happening. At first, you may wonder why so many obstacles are suddenly in your way, or why trouble appeared out of left field, or why you're facing health problems. It often turns out that the trouble you're experiencing is God's means of disciplining you.

When you're a parent, you often need to discipline your children. You do it because you love them and care about what kind of person they're becoming. You also may be concerned about what kind of people your neighbor's children are becoming, but chances are you don't discipline them. Why? They're not your children.

This is why many worldly people have trouble-free lives. "Wherefore do the wicked live, become old, yea, are mighty in power? . . . Their houses are safe from fear, neither is the rod of God upon them" (Job 21:7, 9). Why? Because they're not God's children.

The fact that God goes to the trouble to discipline you proves His love. It may not *seem* that way, but it's the truth. Solomon said, "For whom the Lord loveth he correcteth; even as a father the son in whom he delighteth" (Proverbs 3:12), and Jesus said, "As many as I love, I rebuke and chasten" (Revelation 3:19).

Thou shalt also consider in thine heart, that, as a man chasteneth his son, so the LORD thy God chasteneth thee.

DEUTERONOMY 8:5

And when he was in affliction, he besought the LORD his God, and humbled himself greatly before the God of his fathers.

2 CHRONICLES 33:12

Behold, happy is the man whom God correcteth: therefore despise not thou the chastening of the Almighty.

JOB 5:17

But he knoweth the way that I take: when he hath tried me, I shall come forth as gold.

JOB 23:10

Then he sheweth them their work, and their transgressions that they have exceeded. He openeth also their ear to discipline, and commandeth that they return from iniquity.

JOB 36:9–10

O Lord, rebuke me not in thy wrath: neither chasten me in thy hot displeasure.

PSALM 38:1

It is good for me that I have been afflicted; that I might learn thy statutes.

PSALM 119:71

Remove thy stroke away from me: I am consumed by the blow of thine hand. When thou with rebukes dost correct man for iniquity, thou makest his beauty to consume away like a moth: surely every man is vanity.

PSALM 39:10–11

Blessed is the man whom thou chastenest, O LORD, and teachest him out of thy law; that thou mayest give him rest from the days of adversity.

PSALM 94:12–13

He will not always chide: neither will he keep his anger for ever. He hath not dealt with us after our sins; nor rewarded us according to our iniquities. For as the heaven is high above the earth, so great is his mercy toward them that fear him.

PSALM 103:9–11

Before I was afflicted I went astray: but now have I kept thy word.

PSALM 119:67

My son, despise not the chastening of the LORD; neither be weary of his correction: for whom the LORD loveth he correcteth; even as a father the son in whom he delighteth.

PROVERBS 3:11–12

LORD, in trouble have they visited thee, they poured out a prayer when thy chastening was upon them.

ISAIAH 26:16

*But when we are judged, we are chastened of the Lord,
that we should not be condemned with the world.*

1 CORINTHIANS 11:32

∞

*Though he were a Son, yet learned he obedience by the
things which he suffered.*

HEBREWS 5:8

∞

*And ye have forgotten the exhortation which speaketh unto
you as unto children, My son, despise not thou the chastening of the Lord, nor faint when thou art rebuked of him:
for whom the Lord loveth he chasteneth, and scourgeth
every son whom he receiveth. If ye endure chastening, God
dealeth with you as with sons; for what son is he whom the
father chasteneth not? But if ye be without chastisement,
whereof all are partakers, then are ye bastards, and not
sons. Furthermore we have had fathers of our flesh which
corrected us, and we gave them reverence: shall we not
much rather be in subjection unto the Father of spirits,
and live? For they verily for a few days chastened us after
their own pleasure; but he for our profit, that we might be
partakers of his holiness. Now no chastening for the present
seemeth to be joyous, but grievous: nevertheless afterward
it yieldeth the peaceable fruit of righteousness unto them
which are exercised thereby.*

HEBREWS 12:5–11

∞

*As many as I love, I rebuke and chasten: be zealous
therefore, and repent.*

REVELATION 3:19

19. COMFORT AND ENCOURAGEMENT

God is called "the Father of mercies, and the God of all comfort" (2 Corinthians 1:3). One of the titles of the triune God is "the Comforter" (John 14:26). This quality defines God. First John 4:8 tells you that "God is love," and He often expresses love in gentle, soothing care.

God is the Father who puts His arms around you when you feel alone and abandoned. He is the gentle Jesus, the Friend who sticks closer than a brother when you're distressed. He is the Spirit of consolation that wells up in your heart when you've suffered loss or your dreams have been crushed (Deuteronomy 33:27; Proverbs 18:24).

David declares that "the LORD is nigh unto them that are of a broken heart" (Psalm 34:18). He not only sees your tears and knows the pain in your heart, but is present to bring you peace and to comfort you. He has promised never to leave you or forsake you.

God comforts you in your distress, and He wants you to reach out to others who are suffering and offer them hope and comfort (2 Corinthians 1:3–4). You don't need to be a grief counselor; you don't need to speak fancy words. Sometimes you don't need to speak at all. You just need to *be* there—just like God is for you.

The LORD is nigh unto them that are of a broken heart; and saveth such as be of a contrite spirit.

PSALM 34:18

∞

Thou shalt. . .comfort me on every side.

PSALM 71:21

∞

Shew me a token for good. . .because thou, LORD, hast holpen me, and comforted me.

PSALM 86:17

∞

In the multitude of my thoughts within me thy comforts delight my soul.

PSALM 94:19

∞

Unto the upright there ariseth light in the darkness: he is gracious, and full of compassion, and righteous.

PSALM 112:4

∞

This is my comfort in my affliction: for thy word hath quickened me.

PSALM 119:50

∞

Sing, O heavens; and be joyful, O earth; and break forth into singing, O mountains: for the LORD hath comforted his people, and will have mercy upon his afflicted.

ISAIAH 49:13

I, even I, am he that comforteth you: who art thou, that thou shouldest be afraid of a man that shall die?

ISAIAH 51:12

∽

Surely he hath borne our griefs, and carried our sorrows.

ISAIAH 53:4

∽

As one whom his mother comforteth, so will I comfort you; and ye shall be comforted in Jerusalem.

ISAIAH 66:13

∽

Blessed are they that mourn: for they shall be comforted.

MATTHEW 5:4

∽

And I will pray the Father, and he shall give you another Comforter, that he may abide with you for ever; even the Spirit of truth. . .for he dwelleth with you, and shall be in you. I will not leave you comfortless: I will come to you.

JOHN 14:16–18

∽

Verily, verily, I say unto you, That ye shall weep and lament, but the world shall rejoice: and ye shall be sorrowful, but your sorrow shall be turned into joy.

JOHN 16:20

∽

These things I have spoken unto you, that in me ye might have peace. In the world ye shall have tribulation: but be of good cheer; I have overcome the world.

JOHN 16:33

Then had the churches rest throughout all Judaea and Galilee and Samaria, and were edified; and walking in the fear of the Lord, and in the comfort of the Holy Ghost, were multiplied.

ACTS 9:31

Blessed be God, even the Father of our Lord Jesus Christ, the Father of mercies, and the God of all comfort; who comforteth us in all our tribulation, that we may be able to comfort them which are in any trouble, by the comfort wherewith we ourselves are comforted of God.

2 CORINTHIANS 1:3–4

I am filled with comfort, I am exceeding joyful in all our tribulation.

2 CORINTHIANS 7:4

Nevertheless God, that comforteth those that are cast down, comforted us by the coming of Titus.

2 CORINTHIANS 7:6

And the peace of God, which passeth all understanding, shall keep your hearts and minds through Christ Jesus.

PHILIPPIANS 4:7

That their hearts might be comforted, being knit together in love, and unto all riches of the full assurance of understanding, to the acknowledgement of the mystery of God.

COLOSSIANS 2:2

20. GOD'S PROTECTION

If you're like most believers, you desire for God to protect you and your loved ones from attacks of enemies,
from debilitating accidents, from serious illnesses, and
from financial losses. Realistically, however, you realize
that being God's child is no guarantee that you'll be
spared all this world's woes, because "man is born unto
trouble" (Job 5:7).

Nevertheless, much trouble that comes your way
is avoidable and is *not* God's will for you, so you do
well to be familiar with His promises to protect you.
Many Christians quote Psalm 91—the Protection
Psalm—in times of trouble. This psalm, however, lists
three conditions you must meet if you wish to claim
His protection.

1. You must trust God: "I will say of the LORD,
   He is my refuge and my fortress: my God; in
   him will I trust. Surely he shall deliver thee"
   (vv. 2–3).
2. God must be your constant dwelling place:
   "Because thou hast made the LORD. . .thy
   habitation; there shall no evil befall thee"
   (vv. 9–10).
3. You must love Him deeply: "Because he hath
   set his love upon me, therefore will I deliver
   him" (v. 14).

Only when you meet these conditions is God
obliged to fulfill this promise: "He shall call upon me,
and I will answer him: I will be with him in trouble; I
will deliver him" (v. 15).

The LORD shall fight for you, and ye shall hold your peace.

EXODUS 14:14

The God of my rock; in him will I trust: he is my shield, and the horn of my salvation, my high tower, and my refuge, my saviour; thou savest me from violence.

2 SAMUEL 22:3

But the LORD your God ye shall fear; and he shall deliver you out of the hand of all your enemies.

2 KINGS 17:39

LORD, it is nothing with thee to help, whether with many, or with them that have no power: help us, O LORD our God; for we rest on thee, and in thy name we go against this multitude. O LORD, thou art our God; let no man prevail against thee.

2 CHRONICLES 14:11

Thus saith the LORD unto you, Be not afraid nor dismayed by reason of this great multitude; for the battle is not yours, but God's.

2 CHRONICLES 20:15

Thou art my hiding place; thou shalt preserve me from trouble; thou shalt compass me about with songs of deliverance.

PSALM 32:7

The angel of the LORD encampeth round about them that fear him, and delivereth them.

PSALM 34:7

∞

The righteous cry, and the LORD heareth, and delivereth them out of all their troubles.

PSALM 34:17

∞

And the LORD shall help them, and deliver them: he shall deliver them from the wicked, and save them, because they trust in him.

PSALM 37:40

∞

The LORD will preserve him, and keep him alive; and he shall be blessed upon the earth: and thou wilt not deliver him unto the will of his enemies.

PSALM 41:2

∞

God is our refuge and strength, a very present help in trouble.

PSALM 46:1

∞

When I cry unto thee, then shall mine enemies turn back: this I know; for God is for me.

PSALM 56:9

∞

For the LORD is our defence; and the Holy One of Israel is our king.

PSALM 89:18

The name of the LORD *is a strong tower: the righteous runneth into it, and is safe.*

PROVERBS 18:10

∞

For thou hast been a strength to the poor, a strength to the needy in his distress, a refuge from the storm, a shadow from the heat, when the blast of the terrible ones is as a storm against the wall.

ISAIAH 25:4

∞

Fear thou not; for I am with thee: be not dismayed; for I am thy God: I will strengthen thee; yea, I will help thee; yea, I will uphold thee with the right hand of my righteousness.

ISAIAH 41:10

∞

But I will deliver thee in that day, saith the LORD: *and thou shalt not be given into the hand of the men of whom thou art afraid.*

JEREMIAH 39:17

∞

For the Lord GOD *will help me; therefore shall I not be confounded: therefore have I set my face like a flint, and I know that I shall not be ashamed. He is near that justifieth me; who will contend with me? let us stand together: who is mine adversary? let him come near to me. Behold, the Lord* GOD *will help me; who is he that shall condemn me?*

ISAIAH 50:7–9

21. POWER VERSUS WEAKNESS

Chances are good that, most days, you feel capable of doing your job, navigating life, and managing relationships. And that's a good thing. It shows that God has endowed you with enough of the power, wisdom, knowledge, and skills you need to handle day-to-day matters. But as you've learned, life is often punctuated by those unsettling events called *crises*—circumstances beyond your control, waves bigger than you can handle, problems beyond anyone's ability to solve.

Times like these remind you of how limited and weak you are, of how desperately you need *God's* power. King Jehoshaphat prayed during such a crisis, "O our God. . .we have no might against this great company that cometh against us; neither know we what to do: but our eyes are upon thee" (2 Chronicles 20:12). And David prayed, "Give us help from trouble: for vain is the help of man" (Psalm 60:11).

Problems and emergencies remind you of how incapable you are, but if you let them, they can also remind you that "power belongeth unto God" (Psalm 62:11). It's then that you "seek the Lord, and *his* strength" (Psalm 105:4, emphasis added). You need to be strong during times of great testing, yes, but you are to "be strong in the Lord, and in the power of *his* might" (Ephesians 6:10, emphasis added).

And the LORD said unto Gideon, The people that are with thee are too many for me to give the Midianites into their hands, lest Israel vaunt themselves against me, saying, Mine own hand hath saved me.

JUDGES 7:2

∽

For we are but of yesterday, and know nothing, because our days upon earth are a shadow.

JOB 8:9

∽

He delivered me from my strong enemy, and from them which hated me: for they were too strong for me.

PSALM 18:17

∽

Behold, the nations are as a drop of a bucket, and are counted as the small dust of the balance: behold, he taketh up the isles as a very little thing. . . . All nations before him are as nothing; and they are counted to him less than nothing, and vanity. To whom then will ye liken God? . . . It is he that sitteth upon the circle of the earth, and the inhabitants thereof are as grasshoppers.

ISAIAH 40:15, 17–18, 22

∽

Hast thou not known? hast thou not heard, that the everlasting God, the LORD, the Creator of the ends of the earth, fainteth not, neither is weary? there is no searching of his understanding. He giveth power to the faint; and to them that have no might he increaseth strength.

ISAIAH 40:28–29

*Thus saith the Lord, Let not the wise man glory in his
wisdom, neither let the mighty man glory in his might,
let not the rich man glory in his riches: but let him that
glorieth glory in this, that he understandeth and knoweth
me, that I am the Lord.*

JEREMIAH 9:23–24

∽

*Ah Lord God! behold, thou hast made the heaven and the
earth by thy great power and stretched out arm, and there
is nothing too hard for thee.*

JEREMIAH 32:17

∽

*Behold, I am the Lord, the God of all flesh: is there any
thing too hard for me?*

JEREMIAH 32:27

∽

*I blessed the most High, and I praised and honoured him
that liveth for ever, whose dominion is an everlasting dominion. . .and all the inhabitants of the earth are reputed
as nothing: and he doeth according to his will in the army
of heaven, and among the inhabitants of the earth: and
none can stay his hand, or say unto him, What doest thou?*

DANIEL 4:34–35

∽

*Not by might, nor by power, but by my spirit, saith the
Lord of hosts.*

ZECHARIAH 4:6

With men this is impossible; but with God all things are possible.

MATTHEW 19:26

And Jesus came and spake unto them, saying, All power is given unto me in heaven and in earth.

MATTHEW 28:18

Because the foolishness of God is wiser than men; and the weakness of God is stronger than men. For ye see your calling, brethren, how that not many wise men after the flesh, not many mighty, not many noble, are called: but God hath chosen the foolish things of the world to confound the wise; and God hath chosen the weak things of the world to confound the things which are mighty. . .that no flesh should glory in his presence.

1 CORINTHIANS 1:25–27, 29

And he said unto me, My grace is sufficient for thee: for my strength is made perfect in weakness. Most gladly therefore will I rather glory in my infirmities, that the power of Christ may rest upon me. . . . For when I am weak, then am I strong.

2 CORINTHIANS 12:9–10

22. GOD'S SUPPLY

When Christians experience lack, the first promise many claim is Philippians 4:19, which says, "My God shall supply all your need according to his riches in glory by Christ Jesus." But the Bible contains many promises that God will provide.

In fact, the main lesson that God taught the Israelites in the desert for forty years was that He was able to provide. Nehemiah said, "Thou. . .withheldest not thy manna from their mouth, and gavest them water for their thirst. Yea, forty years didst thou sustain them in the wilderness, so that they lacked nothing" (Nehemiah 9:20–21). They went through serious tests of faith for a time, yes, but overall "they lacked nothing."

You may recall times in your life when you lacked, so you may wonder if you can actually count on God's promises. Consider this: the apostle Paul also experienced lack. He knew what it was like "both to be full and to be hungry, both to abound and to suffer need" (Philippians 4:12). He also admitted, "We both hunger, and thirst, and are naked, and are buffeted, and have no certain dwellingplace" (1 Corinthians 4:11).

Was God failing to supply Paul's needs? No. After allowing him to suffer lack *for a time*—often to test his faith—God then came through and supplied his needs. He never left him destitute.

Moses said, The people, among whom I am, are six hundred thousand footmen; and thou hast said, I will give them flesh, that they may eat a whole month. Shall the flocks and the herds be slain for them, to suffice them? or shall all the fish of the sea be gathered together for them, to suffice them? And the LORD said unto Moses, Is the LORD's hand waxed short? thou shalt see now whether my word shall come to pass unto thee or not.

NUMBERS 11:21–23

∽

The LORD is my shepherd; I shall not want [lack].

PSALM 23:1

∽

O fear the LORD, ye his saints: for there is no want [lack] to them that fear him. The young lions do lack, and suffer hunger: but they that seek the LORD shall not want any good thing.

PSALM 34:9–10

∽

Blessed be the Lord, who daily loadeth us with benefits.

PSALM 68:19

∽

The eyes of all wait upon thee; and thou givest them their meat in due season. Thou openest thine hand, and satisfiest the desire of every living thing.

PSALM 145:15–16

*They said, Can God furnish a table in the wilderness? . . .
Though he had commanded the clouds from above, and
opened the doors of heaven, and had rained down manna
upon them to eat, and had given them of the corn of heaven.
Man did eat angels' food: he sent them meat to the full. He
caused an east wind to blow in the heaven: and by his power
he brought in the south wind. He rained flesh also upon
them as dust, and feathered fowls like as the sand of the sea.*

PSALM 78:19, 23–27

∽

*No good thing will he withhold from them that walk
uprightly.*

PSALM 84:11

∽

*He watereth the hills from his chambers: the earth is
satisfied with the fruit of thy works. He causeth the grass
to grow for the cattle, and herb for the service of man: that
he may bring forth food out of the earth; and wine that
maketh glad the heart of man, and oil to make his face to
shine, and bread which strengtheneth man's heart.*

PSALM 104:13–15

∽

*I will abundantly bless her provision: I will satisfy her
poor with bread.*

PSALM 132:15

∽

*But seek ye first the kingdom of God, and his righteousness;
and all these things shall be added unto you.*

MATTHEW 6:33

Ask, and it shall be given you; seek, and ye shall find; knock, and it shall be opened unto you: for every one that asketh receiveth; and he that seeketh findeth; and to him that knocketh it shall be opened. Or what man is there of you, whom if his son ask bread, will he give him a stone? Or if he ask a fish, will he give him a serpent? If ye then, being evil, know how to give good gifts unto your children, how much more shall your Father which is in heaven give good things to them that ask him?

MATTHEW 7:7–11

∞

Therefore I say unto you, What things soever ye desire, when ye pray, believe that ye receive them, and ye shall have them.

MARK 11:24

∞

He that spared not his own Son, but delivered him up for us all, how shall he not with him also freely give us all things?

ROMANS 8:32

∞

But my God shall supply all your need according to his riches in glory by Christ Jesus.

PHILIPPIANS 4:19

23. GIVING TO GOD

God instituted tithing in the Old Testament, and it was an integral part of the Law of Moses. Moses made it clear that 10 percent of their "increase" went to support the Levites so they could do their work. The entire legal code with its animal sacrifices and purification rituals was supported by tithing. The Jews were also instructed to buy food and drink with their tithes, and to consume this during their annual festivals.

Paul and the writer of Hebrews make it clear, however, that the Mosaic law has been done away with in Christ (Hebrews 8:13; 10:9). Paul declared, "Ye are not under the law, but under grace" (Romans 6:14). This is why some Christians believe that the Old Testament command to tithe is no longer in effect.

They point out that the New Testament gives new guidelines. The Jews were commanded to give 10 percent—it wasn't optional—but Paul instructed Christians, "Every man according as he purposeth in his heart, so let him give; not grudgingly, or of necessity" (2 Corinthians 9:7).

If you are persuaded that you should still tithe, by all means give 10 percent of your income to your church—and do so cheerfully. And if you believe that you're free to decide how much you should give, also give generously and cheerfully, "for God loveth a cheerful giver" (2 Corinthians 9:7).

Take ye from among you an offering unto the LORD:
whosoever is of a willing heart, let him bring it, an
offering of the LORD; gold, and silver, and brass. . . .
And they came, every one whose heart stirred him up,
and every one whom his spirit made willing, and they
brought the LORD's offering to the work of the tabernacle
of the congregation, and for all his service, and for the holy
garments.

EXODUS 35:5, 21

∞

And all the tithe of the land, whether of the seed of the
land, or of the fruit of the tree, is the LORD's: it is holy unto
the LORD.

LEVITICUS 27:30

∞

And concerning the tithe of the herd, or of the flock, even
of whatsoever passeth under the rod, the tenth shall be holy
unto the LORD.

LEVITICUS 27:32

∞

And, behold, I have given the children of Levi all the
tenth in Israel for an inheritance, for their service
which they serve, even the service of the tabernacle of the
congregation. . . . But the tithes of the children of Israel,
which they offer as an heave offering unto the LORD, I have
given to the Levites to inherit.

NUMBERS 18:21, 24

Thou shalt truly tithe all the increase of thy seed, that the field bringeth forth year by year. And thou shalt eat before the LORD thy God, in the place which he shall choose to place his name there, the tithe of thy corn, of thy wine, and of thine oil, and the firstlings of thy herds and of thy flocks. . . . And if the way be too long for thee. . .then shalt thou turn it into money, and bind up the money in thine hand, and shalt go unto the place which the LORD thy God shall choose: and thou shalt bestow that money for whatsoever thy soul lusteth after, for oxen, or for sheep, or for wine, or for strong drink, or for whatsoever thy soul desireth: and thou shalt eat there before the LORD thy God, and thou shalt rejoice, thou, and thine household.

DEUTERONOMY 14:22–26

∞

But who am I, and what is my people, that we should be able to offer so willingly after this sort? for all things come of thee, and of thine own have we given thee.

1 CHRONICLES 29:14

∞

Will a man rob God? Yet ye have robbed me. But ye say, Wherein have we robbed thee? In tithes and offerings. Ye are cursed with a curse: for ye have robbed me, even this whole nation. Bring ye all the tithes into the storehouse, that there may be meat in mine house, and prove me now herewith, saith the LORD of hosts, if I will not open you the windows of heaven, and pour you out a blessing, that there shall not be room enough to receive it.

MALACHI 3:8–10

Honour the LORD with thy substance, and with the firstfruits of all thine increase: so shall thy barns be filled with plenty, and thy presses shall burst out with new wine.

PROVERBS 3:9–10

∽

Upon the first day of the week let every one of you lay by him in store, as God hath prospered him, that there be no gatherings when I come.

1 CORINTHIANS 16:2

∽

Every man according as he purposeth in his heart, so let him give; not grudgingly, or of necessity: for God loveth a cheerful giver.

2 CORINTHIANS 9:7

24. WEALTH AND POVERTY

There's some confusion surrounding the subject of prosperity. Some people, for example, follow prosperity doctrines that teach that one of the surest signs you're righteous is if you're being blessed with material riches. Paul declares this doctrine "destitute of the truth, supposing that gain is godliness" (1 Timothy 6:5).

However, you're not necessarily godlier if you're poor. That's why Agur prayed, "Give me neither poverty nor riches. . .lest I be full, and deny thee, and say, Who is the LORD? or lest I be poor, and steal, and take the name of my God in vain" (Proverbs 30:8–9).

Paul experienced both abundance and lack, and declared, "I have learned, in whatsoever state I am, therewith to be content. I know both how to be abased, and I know how to abound" (Philippians 4:11–12). The most important thing is that you possess spiritual riches. If you do, your financial status is neither here nor there. Solomon observed, "There is that maketh himself rich, yet hath nothing: there is that maketh himself poor, yet hath great riches" (Proverbs 13:7).

If a righteous person has studied hard and worked hard to obtain prosperity, good for him or her. So long as he or she isn't overfocusing on career to the detriment of spiritual health or family relationships, there's nothing wrong with being prosperous.

But thou shalt remember the LORD thy God: for it is he that giveth thee power to get wealth.

DEUTERONOMY 8:18

If there be among you a poor man. . .thou shalt open thine hand wide unto him, and shalt surely lend him sufficient for his need, in that which he wanteth. . . . Thou shalt surely give him, and thine heart shall not be grieved when thou givest unto him: because that for this thing the LORD thy God shall bless thee in all thy works, and in all that thou puttest thine hand unto.

DEUTERONOMY 15:7–8, 10

This book of the law shall not depart out of thy mouth; but thou shalt meditate therein day and night, that thou mayest observe to do according to all that is written therein: for then thou shalt make thy way prosperous, and then thou shalt have good success.

JOSHUA 1:8

If riches increase, set not your heart upon them.

PSALM 62:10

∞

Blessed is the man that feareth the LORD, that delighteth greatly in his commandments. . . . Wealth and riches shall be in his house: and his righteousness endureth for ever.

PSALM 112:1, 3

The blessing of the LORD, it maketh rich, and he addeth no sorrow with it.

PROVERBS 10:22

∞

Wealth gotten by vanity shall be diminished: but he that gathereth by labour shall increase.

PROVERBS 13:11

∞

Wilt thou set thine eyes upon that which is not? for riches certainly make themselves wings; they fly away as an eagle toward heaven.

PROVERBS 23:5

∞

He that tilleth his land shall have plenty of bread: but he that followeth after vain persons shall have poverty enough.

PROVERBS 28:19

∞

No man can serve two masters: for either he will hate the one, and love the other; or else he will hold to the one, and despise the other. Ye cannot serve God and mammon.

MATTHEW 6:24

∞

Let him that stole steal no more: but rather let him labour, working with his hands the thing which is good, that he may have to give to him that needeth.

EPHESIANS 4:28

*Love not sleep, lest thou come to poverty; open thine eyes,
and thou shalt be satisfied with bread.*

PROVERBS 20:13

∞

*And that ye study to be quiet, and to do your own business,
and to work with your own hands, as we commanded you;
that ye may walk honestly toward them that are without,
and that ye may have lack of nothing.*

1 THESSALONIANS 4:11–12

∞

*For even when we were with you, this we commanded you,
that if any would not work, neither should he eat. For we
hear that there are some which walk among you disorderly,
working not at all, but are busybodies. Now them that are
such we command and exhort by our Lord Jesus Christ,
that with quietness they work, and eat their own bread.*

2 THESSALONIANS 3:10-12

∞

*But they that will be rich fall into temptation and a snare,
and into many foolish and hurtful lusts, which drown men
in destruction and perdition. For the love of money is the
root of all evil: which while some coveted after, they have
erred from the faith, and pierced themselves through with
many sorrows.*

1 TIMOTHY 6:9–10

∞

*And let ours also learn to maintain good works for
necessary uses, that they be not unfruitful.*

TITUS 3:14

25. DILIGENCE AND FAITHFULNESS

Diligent means "showing care and conscientiousness in one's duties," and *diligence* means "careful and persistent effort." Diligent people don't do haphazard work; they don't slack off; they put forth extra effort to ensure that a job has been done right—and do so consistently.

Diligent people pay attention; they investigate irregularities; they look into things; they check out accounts; and they do their homework. In a legal sense, "performing due diligence" refers to "the care that a reasonable person exercises to avoid harm to other persons or their property." Why do diligent people continually go the extra mile? Because they *care*.

Another word for *diligent* is *faithful*. Matthew 24:45–46 says: "Who then is a faithful and wise servant, whom his lord hath made ruler over his household, to give them meat in due season? Blessed is that servant, whom his lord when he cometh shall find so doing." That's another thing about diligent people. They perform their duties "in due season"—on time, punctually, and exactly the way they're supposed to.

Joseph and Daniel are often cited as men who were diligent in everything they did, and—as a result—were promoted to positions of trust and authority. Another such man was Timothy. Paul said that Timothy had "proved himself" (see Philippians 2:22). Are you diligent? Do you prove yourself?

*And the L*ORD *was with Joseph, and he was a prosperous man; and he was in the house of his master the Egyptian. And his master saw that the L*ORD *was with him, and that the L*ORD *made all that he did to prosper in his hand. And Joseph found grace in his sight, and he served him: and he made him overseer over his house, and all that he had he put into his hand. And it came to pass from the time that he had made him overseer in his house, and over all that he had, that the L*ORD *blessed the Egyptian's house for Joseph's sake; and the blessing of the L*ORD *was upon all that he had in the house, and in the field. And he left all that he had in Joseph's hand; and he knew not ought he had, save the bread which he did eat.*

GENESIS 39:2–6

Howbeit there was no reckoning made with them of the money that was delivered into their hand, because they dealt faithfully.

2 KINGS 22:7

It pleased Darius to set over the kingdom an hundred and twenty princes, which should be over the whole kingdom; and over these three presidents; of whom Daniel was first. . . . Then the presidents and princes sought to find occasion against Daniel concerning the kingdom; but they could find none occasion nor fault; forasmuch as he was faithful, neither was there any error or fault found in him.

DANIEL 6:1–2, 4

A faithful man shall abound with blessings: but he that maketh haste to be rich shall not be innocent.

PROVERBS 28:20

∞

He becometh poor that dealeth with a slack hand: but the hand of the diligent maketh rich.

PROVERBS 10:4

∞

The hand of the diligent shall bear rule.

PROVERBS 12:24

∞

The thoughts of the diligent tend only to plenteousness; but of every one that is hasty only to want.

PROVERBS 21:5

∞

Seest thou a man diligent in his business? he shall stand before kings; he shall not stand before mean men.

PROVERBS 22:29

∞

Be thou diligent to know the state of thy flocks, and look well to thy herds.

PROVERBS 27:23

∞

Who then is a faithful and wise servant, whom his lord hath made ruler over his household, to give them meat in due season? Blessed is that servant, whom his lord when he cometh shall find so doing.

MATTHEW 24:45–46

His lord said unto him, Well done, good and faithful servant; thou hast been faithful over a few things, I will make thee ruler over many things: enter thou into the joy of thy lord.

MATTHEW 25:23

He that is faithful in that which is least is faithful also in much: and he that is unjust in the least is unjust also in much. If therefore ye have not been faithful in the unrighteous mammon, who will commit to your trust the true riches? And if ye have not been faithful in that which is another man's, who shall give you that which is your own?

LUKE 16:10–12

Having then gifts differing according to the grace that is given to us, whether. . .ministry, let us wait on our ministering: or he that teacheth, on teaching; or he that exhorteth, on exhortation: he that giveth, let him do it with simplicity; he that ruleth, with diligence.

ROMANS 12:6–8

Moreover it is required in stewards, that a man be found faithful.

1 CORINTHIANS 4:2

26. CONTENTMENT VERSUS GREED

The apostle Paul declared, "We brought nothing into this world, and it is certain we can carry nothing out. And having food and raiment let us be therewith content" (1 Timothy 6:7–8). What was the secret of Paul's contentment? He followed his own advice, which was this: "Set your affection on things above, not on things on the earth" (Colossians 3:2).

The writer of Hebrews explained the attitude that brings contentment: "Be content with such things as ye have: for he hath said, I will never leave thee, nor forsake thee" (Hebrews 13:5). Believers can be content with little because they have "God, who giveth us richly all things to enjoy" (1 Timothy 6:17).

Greed is the opposite of contentment. A contented man has peace, but "he that is greedy of gain troubleth his own house" (Proverbs 15:27). Too many people have their eyes focused on the things of this world. James said, "For the sun is no sooner risen with a burning heat, but it withereth the grass, and the flower thereof falleth. . .so also shall the rich man fade away" (James 1:11).

Jesus' disciples were described "as poor, yet making many rich; as having nothing, and yet possessing all things" (2 Corinthians 6:10). What they lacked in earthly riches, they made up for in the abundance of their spiritual wealth.

But as for me, my feet were almost gone; my steps had well nigh slipped. For I was envious at the foolish, when I saw the prosperity of the wicked.

PSALM 73:2–3

Wilt thou set thine eyes upon that which is not? for riches certainly make themselves wings; they fly away as an eagle toward heaven.

PROVERBS 23:5

There is a sore evil which I have seen under the sun, namely, riches kept for the owners thereof to their hurt. But those riches perish by evil travail: and he begetteth a son, and there is nothing in his hand. As he came forth of his mother's womb, naked shall he return to go as he came, and shall take nothing of his labour, which he may carry away in his hand.

ECCLESIASTES 5:13–15

But lay up for yourselves treasures in heaven, where neither moth nor rust doth corrupt, and where thieves do not break through nor steal: for where your treasure is, there will your heart be also.

MATTHEW 6:20–21

In every thing give thanks: for this is the will of God in Christ Jesus concerning you.

1 THESSALONIANS 5:18

He also that received seed among the thorns is he that heareth the word; and the care of this world, and the deceitfulness of riches, choke the word, and he becometh unfruitful.

MATTHEW 13:22

Children, how hard is it for them that trust in riches to enter into the kingdom of God! It is easier for a camel to go through the eye of a needle, than for a rich man to enter into the kingdom of God.

MARK 10:24–25

Although the fig tree shall not blossom, neither shall fruit be in the vines; the labour of the olive shall fail, and the fields shall yield no meat; the flock shall be cut off from the fold, and there shall be no herd in the stalls: yet I will rejoice in the LORD, I will joy in the God of my salvation.

HABAKKUK 3:17–18

And he said unto them, Take heed, and beware of covetousness: for a man's life consisteth not in the abundance of the things which he possesseth.

LUKE 12:15

Perverse disputings of men of corrupt minds, and destitute of the truth, supposing that gain is godliness: from such withdraw thyself.

1 TIMOTHY 6:5

For we brought nothing into this world, and it is certain we can carry nothing out. And having food and raiment let us be therewith content.

1 TIMOTHY 6:7–8

For the love of money is the root of all evil: which while some coveted after, they have erred from the faith, and pierced themselves through with many sorrows.

1 TIMOTHY 6:10

Charge them that are rich in this world, that they be not highminded, nor trust in uncertain riches, but in the living God, who giveth us richly all things to enjoy.

1 TIMOTHY 6:17

For ye. . .took joyfully the spoiling of your goods, knowing in yourselves that ye have in heaven a better and an enduring substance.

HEBREWS 10:34

Let your conversation [lifestyle] be without covetousness; and be content with such things as ye have: for he hath said, I will never leave thee, nor forsake thee.

HEBREWS 13:5

Because thou sayest, I am rich, and increased with goods, and have need of nothing; and knowest not that thou art wretched, and miserable, and poor, and blind, and naked.

REVELATION 3:17

27. HAPPINESS AND JOY

When the Jews were rebuilding the wall around Jerusalem, the work was so overwhelming that they groaned, "The strength of the bearers of burdens is decayed" (Nehemiah 4:10). Worse yet, as Nehemiah said, "They all [enemies] made us afraid, saying, Their hands shall be weakened from the work, that it be not done. Now therefore, O God, strengthen my hands" (Nehemiah 6:9).

How did God strengthen the Jews? He sent them *joy*! Nehemiah 8:10 declares, "The joy of the LORD is your strength." His joy undergirds you and keeps you going when you feel like collapsing. Joy is vital.

Many people think joy is the same as peace, only with a bigger smile. But those are separate fruits of the Spirit (Galatians 5:22). To be joyful is to be happy— *very* happy. David wrote, "Let all those that put their trust in thee rejoice: let them ever *shout* for joy" (Psalm 5:11, emphasis added). But you don't have to be shouting to have the joy of the Lord. You can laugh instead. Or have a smile so big it could button in back. But joy is definitely more animated than peace.

If you're lacking joy, the solution is to spend more time in the presence of God because, as David said, "in [God's] presence is fulness of joy" (Psalm 16:11).

For this day is holy unto our LORD: neither be ye sorry; for the joy of the LORD is your strength.

NEHEMIAH 8:10

∞

Behold, happy is the man whom God correcteth: therefore despise not thou the chastening of the Almighty.

JOB 5:17

∞

But let all those that put their trust in thee rejoice: let them ever shout for joy, because thou defendest them: let them also that love thy name be joyful in thee.

PSALM 5:11

∞

Thou wilt shew me the path of life: in thy presence is fulness of joy; at thy right hand there are pleasures for evermore.

PSALM 16:11

∞

For his anger endureth but a moment; in his favour is life: weeping may endure for a night, but joy cometh in the morning.

PSALM 30:5

∞

Be glad in the LORD, and rejoice, ye righteous: and shout for joy, all ye that are upright in heart.

PSALM 32:11

∞

And my soul shall be joyful in the LORD: it shall rejoice in his salvation.

PSALM 35:9

Restore unto me the joy of thy salvation; and uphold me with thy free spirit.

PSALM 51:12

∞

Make a joyful noise unto the LORD, all the earth: make a loud noise, and rejoice, and sing praise.

PSALM 98:4

∞

That our sons may be as plants grown up in their youth; that our daughters may be as corner stones, polished after the similitude of a palace: that our garners may be full, affording all manner of store: that our sheep may bring forth thousands and ten thousands in our streets: that our oxen may be strong to labour; that there be no breaking in, nor going out; that there be no complaining in our streets. Happy is that people, that is in such a case: yea, happy is that people, whose God is the LORD.

PSALM 144:12–15

∞

Happy is he that hath the God of Jacob for his help, whose hope is in the LORD his God.

PSALM 146:5

∞

Happy is the man that findeth wisdom, and the man that getteth understanding.

PROVERBS 3:13

∞

A merry heart maketh a cheerful countenance: but by sorrow of the heart the spirit is broken.

PROVERBS 15:13

All the days of the afflicted are evil: but he that is of a merry heart hath a continual feast.

PROVERBS 15:15

A merry heart doeth good like a medicine: but a broken spirit drieth the bones.

PROVERBS 17:22

Therefore the redeemed of the LORD shall return, and come with singing unto Zion; and everlasting joy shall be upon their head: they shall obtain gladness and joy; and sorrow and mourning shall flee away.

ISAIAH 51:11

These things have I spoken unto you, that my joy might remain in you, and that your joy might be full.

JOHN 15:11

For the kingdom of God is. . .righteousness, and peace, and joy in the Holy Ghost.

ROMANS 14:17

But the fruit of the Spirit is love, joy, peace, longsuffering, gentleness, goodness, faith, meekness, temperance.

GALATIANS 5:22–23

Rejoice in the Lord always: and again I say, Rejoice.

PHILIPPIANS 4:4

28. PEACE

So many people in the world lack peace. They're unsettled, troubled, worried, and plagued by a guilty conscience. They condemn themselves for their failures and beat themselves up over their sins. But Jesus came to bring peace between the Father and humanity. One of His many titles is "Prince of Peace" (Isaiah 9:6). God "made peace through the blood of his cross, by him [Jesus] to reconcile all things unto himself" (Colossians 1:20).

But even many Christians lack peace. Sometimes this is because they have sin in their lives that they aren't willing to repent of and forsake. But more often than not, it's because the devil, "the accuser of our brethren" (Revelation 12:10), has so beaten them down that he has them convinced that, although God may forgive others, He won't forgive *them*. That's a lie.

Job 22:21 says, "Acquaint now thyself with him, and be at peace." If you've never asked God to forgive you and to send the Spirit of His Son into your heart, do it now. If you already know God, get better acquainted with Him. Know that He loves you and forgives you. "And the peace of God. . .shall keep your hearts and minds through Christ Jesus" (Philippians 4:7).

Peace is a blessing from God. Experience His peace today. "The LORD bless thee. . .and give thee peace" (Numbers 6:24, 26).

And he said, My presence shall go with thee, and I will give thee rest.

EXODUS 33:14

∽

The LORD bless thee, and keep thee: the LORD make his face shine upon thee, and be gracious unto thee: the LORD lift up his countenance upon thee, and give thee peace.

NUMBERS 6:24–26

∽

And the LORD said unto him, Peace be unto thee; fear not: thou shalt not die.

JUDGES 6:23

∽

And thus shall ye say to him that liveth in prosperity, Peace be both to thee, and peace be to thine house, and peace be unto all that thou hast.

1 SAMUEL 25:6

∽

Acquaint now thyself with him, and be at peace: thereby good shall come unto thee.

JOB 22:21

∽

I will both lay me down in peace, and sleep: for thou, LORD, only makest me dwell in safety.

PSALM 4:8

∽

There is no peace, saith my God, to the wicked.

ISAIAH 57:21

The LORD will give strength unto his people; the LORD will bless his people with peace.

PSALM 29:11

∞

I will hear what God the LORD will speak: for he will speak peace unto his people, and to his saints.

PSALM 85:8

∞

He shall not be afraid of evil tidings: his heart is fixed, trusting in the LORD. His heart is established, he shall not be afraid, until he see his desire upon his enemies.

PSALM 112:7–8

∞

Great peace have they which love thy law: and nothing shall offend them.

PSALM 119:165

∞

Thou wilt keep him in perfect peace, whose mind is stayed on thee: because he trusteth in thee.

ISAIAH 26:3

∞

LORD, thou wilt ordain peace for us: for thou also hast wrought all our works in us.

ISAIAH 26:12

∞

For ye shall go out with joy, and be led forth with peace.

ISAIAH 55:12

These things I have spoken unto you, that in me ye might have peace. In the world ye shall have tribulation: but be of good cheer; I have overcome the world.

JOHN 16:33

∽

Therefore being justified by faith, we have peace with God through our Lord Jesus Christ.

ROMANS 5:1

∽

Now the God of hope fill you with all joy and peace in believing, that ye may abound in hope.

ROMANS 15:13

∽

Now the God of peace be with you all. Amen.

ROMANS 15:33

∽

For God is not the author of confusion, but of peace.

1 CORINTHIANS 14:33

∽

Grace be to you, and peace, from God our Father, and from the Lord Jesus Christ.

EPHESIANS 1:2

∽

And the peace of God, which passeth all understanding, shall keep your hearts and minds through Christ Jesus.

PHILIPPIANS 4:7

29. COURAGE VERSUS FEAR

We all experience fear at times. Even the faith-filled apostle Paul said that on one trip to Greece, "we were troubled on every side; without were fightings, within were fears" (2 Corinthians 7:5). The mighty warrior David confessed that he too experienced fear—but he also gave the solution: "What time I am afraid, I will trust in thee" (Psalm 56:3). How did he gain courage? When fear swept in, David put his trust in God and held firmly to Him.

Jesus told a Jew named Jairus, "Be not afraid, only believe" (Mark 5:36). The more you trust God and focus on His power to work miracles on your behalf, the less fear you'll have. Faith conquers fear.

God told His people throughout the Bible, "Be not afraid" (see Joshua 1:9; 2 Kings 19:6). You can make a choice to not fear. Sometimes you may feel like you have little control over your fears. You may feel like the psalmist who said, "Fearfulness and trembling are come upon me, and horror hath overwhelmed me." But even though he *felt* overwhelmed, he went on to say, "As for me, I will call upon God; and the LORD shall save me." Sure enough, he later rejoiced, saying, "He hath delivered my soul in peace from the battle that was against me" (Psalm 55:5, 16, 18).

*But it shall come to pass, if thou wilt not hearken unto the
voice of the L*ORD *thy God. . . . the L*ORD *shall give thee
there a trembling heart, and failing of eyes, and sorrow of
mind: and thy life shall hang in doubt before thee; and thou
shalt fear day and night, and shalt have none assurance of
thy life: in the morning thou shalt say, Would God it were
even! and at even thou shalt say, Would God it were morning! for the fear of thine heart wherewith thou shalt fear,
and for the sight of thine eyes which thou shalt see.*

DEUTERONOMY 28:15, 65–67

∽

*Have not I commanded thee? Be strong and of a good cour-
age; be not afraid, neither be thou dismayed: for the L*ORD
thy God is with thee whithersoever thou goest.

JOSHUA 1:9

∽

*Be not afraid of the words which thou hast heard, with which
the servants of the king of Assyria have blasphemed me.*

2 KINGS 19:6

∽

*I will not be afraid of ten thousands of people, that have set
themselves against me round about.*

PSALM 3:6

∽

*The L*ORD *is my light and my salvation; whom shall I
fear? the L*ORD *is the strength of my life; of whom shall I be
afraid? . . . Though an host should encamp against me, my
heart shall not fear: though war should rise against me, in
this will I be confident.*

PSALM 27:1, 3

God is our refuge and strength, a very present help in trouble. Therefore will not we fear, though the earth be removed, and though the mountains be carried into the midst of the sea.

PSALM 46:1–2

∞

Fearfulness and trembling are come upon me, and horror hath overwhelmed me. . . . As for me, I will call upon God; and the LORD shall save me. Evening, and morning, and at noon, will I pray, and cry aloud: and he shall hear my voice. He hath delivered my soul in peace from the battle that was against me.

PSALM 55:5, 16–18

∞

What time I am afraid, I will trust in thee. In God I will praise his word, in God I have put my trust; I will not fear what flesh can do unto me.

PSALM 56:3–4

∞

The LORD is on my side; I will not fear: what can man do unto me?

PSALM 118:6

∞

The fear of the wicked, it shall come upon him.

PROVERBS 10:24

∞

Behold, God is my salvation; I will trust, and not be afraid.

ISAIAH 12:2

I, even I, am he that comforteth you: who art thou, that thou shouldest be afraid of a man that shall die, and of the son of man which shall be made as grass; and forgettest the LORD thy maker. . .and hast feared continually every day because of the fury of the oppressor, as if he were ready to destroy? and where is the fury of the oppressor?

ISAIAH 51:12–13

∞

Why are ye so fearful? how is it that ye have no faith?

MARK 4:40

∞

For God hath not given us the spirit of fear; but of power, and of love, and of a sound mind.

2 TIMOTHY 1:7

∞

So that we may boldly say, The Lord is my helper, and I will not fear what man shall do unto me.

HEBREWS 13:6

∞

There is no fear in love; but perfect love casteth out fear: because fear hath torment. He that feareth is not made perfect in love.

1 JOHN 4:18

30. PATIENCE AND LONG-SUFFERING

Patience and long-suffering are related but different. You need patience if you're required to wait for something. Even standing in line to pay for groceries requires patience. The main obstacle you need to overcome in such situations is boredom or the feeling that you're wasting your time.

The Bible frequently admonishes believers to "rest in the LORD, and wait patiently for him" (Psalm 37:7) and to "[wait] patiently for the LORD" (Psalm 40:1).

God often takes longer to answer prayers than you think He should—especially if you're going through troubling times. That's why Paul advises Christians to be "patient in tribulation" (Romans 12:12). Earlier, Paul said that "tribulation worketh patience" (Romans 5:3). In modern English that means "suffering produces perseverance." God wants you to have patience, and usually the only way you get it is by enduring troubles.

Long-suffering also requires patience, but it's specifically speaking about having patience when dealing with difficult circumstances or aggravating people. For example, teaching children requires patience. Sometimes it also requires long-suffering because you will *suffer* a *long* time, patiently putting up with wrong attitudes or immature behavior. *Long-suffering* is defined as "having patience in spite of troubles, especially those caused by other people."

Colossians 3:12–13 says that Christians are to be known for "forbearing one another"—in other words, "putting up with one another."

The LORD is longsuffering, and of great mercy, forgiving iniquity and transgression.

NUMBERS 14:18

∽

Rest in the LORD, and wait patiently for him.

PSALM 37:7

∽

I waited patiently for the LORD; and he inclined unto me, and heard my cry.

PSALM 40:1

∽

Better is the end of a thing than the beginning thereof: and the patient in spirit is better than the proud in spirit.

ECCLESIASTES 7:8

∽

But that on the good ground are they, which in an honest and good heart, having heard the word, keep it, and bring forth fruit with patience.

LUKE 8:15

∽

In your patience possess ye your souls.

LUKE 21:19

∽

Who will render to every man according to his deeds: to them who by patient continuance in well doing seek for glory and honour and immortality, eternal life.

ROMANS 2:6–7

And not only so, but we glory in tribulations also: knowing that tribulation worketh patience; and patience, experience; and experience, hope.

ROMANS 5:3–4

∞

But if we hope for that we see not, then do we with patience wait for it.

ROMANS 8:25

∞

Rejoicing in hope; patient in tribulation; continuing instant in prayer.

ROMANS 12:12

∞

But in all things approving ourselves as the ministers of God, in much patience, in afflictions, in necessities, in distresses.

2 CORINTHIANS 6:4

∞

But the fruit of the Spirit is love, joy, peace, longsuffering, gentleness, goodness, faith.

GALATIANS 5:22

∞

Put on therefore, as the elect of God, holy and beloved, bowels of mercies, kindness, humbleness of mind, meekness, longsuffering; forbearing one another, and forgiving one another, if any man have a quarrel against any: even as Christ forgave you, so also do ye.

COLOSSIANS 3:12–13

So that we ourselves glory in you in the churches of God for your patience and faith in all your persecutions and tribulations that ye endure.

2 THESSALONIANS 1:4

∞

And the servant of the Lord must not strive; but be gentle unto all men, apt to teach, patient.

2 TIMOTHY 2:24

∞

That ye be not slothful, but followers of them who through faith and patience inherit the promises.

HEBREWS 6:12

∞

And so, after he had patiently endured, he obtained the promise.

HEBREWS 6:15

∞

For ye have need of patience, that, after ye have done the will of God, ye might receive the promise.

HEBREWS 10:36

∞

Wherefore seeing we also are compassed about with so great a cloud of witnesses, let us lay aside every weight, and the sin which doth so easily beset us, and let us run with patience the race that is set before us.

HEBREWS 12:1

∞

Knowing this, that the trying of your faith worketh patience. But let patience have her perfect work, that ye may be perfect and entire, wanting nothing.

JAMES 1:3–4

31. HOPE VERSUS DESPAIR

The apostle Peter wrote that Christians have not only "hope" but a "lively hope" of heaven, so they can be joyful even in troubled times (see 1 Peter 1:3–6). It's true. Knowing that you have heaven to look forward to can buoy you up during dark times. However, when you've been experiencing difficulties for some time and it seems like there's no end in sight, you can begin to lose hope that things will ever get better.

David said, "I had fainted, unless I had believed to see the goodness of the Lord in the land of the living" (Psalm 27:13). It's wonderful to have a heavenly hope, but you *also* need to believe that you'll once again experience "the goodness of the Lord in the land of the living," in the here and now.

How do you get hope when you're sinking in depression? Paul wrote, "The God of hope fill you with all joy and peace. . .that ye may abound in hope" (Romans 15:13). Hope is born of joy and peace. So pray for God to fill you with joy and peace.

David was very emotional, and one time when he was depressed, he told his soul to "hope in God: for I shall yet praise him" (Psalm 43:5). Sometimes you too need to declare, "I'm going to trust God!"

I had fainted, unless I had believed to see the goodness of the LORD in the land of the living.

PSALM 27:13

∽

Be of good courage, and he shall strengthen your heart, all ye that hope in the LORD.

PSALM 31:24

∽

Behold, the eye of the LORD is upon them that fear him, upon them that hope in his mercy.

PSALM 33:18

∽

Let thy mercy, O LORD, be upon us, according as we hope in thee.

PSALM 33:22

∽

I am feeble and sore broken: I have roared by reason of the disquietness of my heart. Lord, all my desire is before thee; and my groaning is not hid from thee.

PSALM 38:8–9

∽

For in thee, O LORD, do I hope: thou wilt hear, O Lord my God.

PSALM 38:15

∽

Remember the word unto thy servant, upon which thou hast caused me to hope.

PSALM 119:49

Why art thou cast down, O my soul? and why art thou disquieted within me? hope in God: for I shall yet praise him, who is the health of my countenance, and my God.

PSALM 43:5

∞

I wait for the LORD, my soul doth wait, and in his word do I hope.

PSALM 130:5

∞

Let Israel hope in the LORD: for with the LORD there is mercy, and with him is plenteous redemption.

PSALM 130:7

∞

Happy is he that hath the God of Jacob for his help, whose hope is in the LORD his God.

PSALM 146:5

∞

The LORD taketh pleasure in them that fear him, in those that hope in his mercy.

PSALM 147:11

∞

Hope deferred maketh the heart sick: but when the desire cometh, it is a tree of life.

PROVERBS 13:12

∞

The LORD is my portion, saith my soul; therefore will I hope in him.

LAMENTATIONS 3:24

It is good that a man should both hope and quietly wait for the salvation of the LORD.

LAMENTATIONS 3:26

⊷⊷

Come unto me, all ye that labour and are heavy laden, and I will give you rest. Take my yoke upon you, and learn of me; for I am meek and lowly in heart: and ye shall find rest unto your souls. For my yoke is easy, and my burden is light.

MATTHEW 11:28–30

⊷⊷

For we would not, brethren, have you ignorant of our trouble which came to us in Asia, that we were pressed out of measure, above strength, insomuch that we despaired even of life.

2 CORINTHIANS 1:8

⊷⊷

We are troubled on every side, yet not distressed; we are perplexed, but not in despair.

2 CORINTHIANS 4:8

⊷⊷

Who against hope believed in hope, that he might become the father of many nations.

ROMANS 4:18

⊷⊷

Now the God of hope fill you with all joy and peace in believing, that ye may abound in hope, through the power of the Holy Ghost.

ROMANS 15:13

32. LOVING OTHERS

The command to love others is stressed repeatedly in both the Old and New Testaments. The Israelites were told, "Thou shalt love thy neighbour as thyself" (Leviticus 19:18). When a lawyer (a scribe) asked Jesus, "And who is my neighbour?" he was asking Jesus to tell him who *exactly* he *had* to love so he could know who he didn't need to bother loving. Jesus basically told him that his neighbor was anyone who needed his help. He was to love everyone.

You may not wonder what "neighbour" means, but you may wonder exactly what is meant by "love." The apostle Paul gave the answer in his epistle to the Corinthians. (I've substituted "love" for "charity" in the following verses, because to most modern people, "charity" means only money given to the poor.) Paul wrote:

"[Love] suffereth long, and is kind; [love] envieth not; [love] vaunteth not itself, is not puffed up, doth not behave itself unseemly, seeketh not her own, is not easily provoked, thinketh no evil; rejoiceth not in iniquity, but rejoiceth in the truth; beareth all things, believeth all things, hopeth all things, endureth all things. [Love] never faileth" (1 Corinthians 13:4–8).

Do you want to show real, genuine love to others? Then read the list above and check whether you're loving them according to the Bible's definition.

Thou shalt not avenge, nor bear any grudge against the children of thy people, but thou shalt love thy neighbour as thyself: I am the LORD.

LEVITICUS 19:18

Love your enemies, bless them that curse you, do good to them that hate you, and pray for them which despitefully use you, and persecute you.

MATTHEW 5:44

Jesus said unto him, Thou shalt love the Lord thy God with all thy heart, and with all thy soul, and with all thy mind. This is the first and great commandment. And the second is like unto it, Thou shalt love thy neighbour as thyself. On these two commandments hang all the law and the prophets.

MATTHEW 22:37–40

And, behold, a certain lawyer stood up, and tempted him, saying, Master, what shall I do to inherit eternal life? He said unto him, What is written in the law? how readest thou? And he answering said, Thou shalt love the Lord thy God with all thy heart, and with all thy soul, and with all thy strength, and with all thy mind; and thy neighbour as thyself. And he said unto him, Thou hast answered right: this do, and thou shalt live. But he, willing to justify himself, said unto Jesus, And who is my neighbour? . . . Which now of these three, thinkest thou, was neighbour unto him that fell among the thieves? And he said, He that shewed mercy on him. Then said Jesus unto him, Go, and do thou likewise.

LUKE 10:25–29, 36–37

A new commandment I give unto you, That ye love one another; as I have loved you, that ye also love one another. By this shall all men know that ye are my disciples, if ye have love one to another.

JOHN 13:34–35

∞

For this, Thou shalt not commit adultery, Thou shalt not kill, Thou shalt not steal, Thou shalt not bear false witness, Thou shalt not covet; and if there be any other commandment, it is briefly comprehended in this saying, namely, Thou shalt love thy neighbour as thyself. Love worketh no ill to his neighbour: therefore love is the fulfilling of the law.

ROMANS 13:9–10

∞

And above all things have fervent charity among yourselves: for charity shall cover the multitude of sins.

1 PETER 4:8

∞

Hereby perceive we the love of God, because he laid down his life for us: and we ought to lay down our lives for the brethren.

1 JOHN 3:16

∞

But whoso hath this world's good, and seeth his brother have need, and shutteth up his bowels of compassion from him, how dwelleth the love of God in him? My little children, let us not love in word, neither in tongue; but in deed and in truth.

1 JOHN 3:17–18

And this is his commandment, That we should believe on the name of his Son Jesus Christ, and love one another, as he gave us commandment.

1 JOHN 3:23

If a man say, I love God, and hateth his brother, he is a liar: for he that loveth not his brother whom he hath seen, how can he love God whom he hath not seen?

1 JOHN 4:20

33. FORGIVING OTHERS

The prophet Micah declared to the Israelites, "He hath shewed thee, O man, what is good; and what doth the LORD require of thee, but. . .to love mercy?" (Micah 6:8). God is very clear about what He requires. He insists that you are "to *love* mercy." Why? Because mercy is good.

What would change in your life if you had a passionate love for mercy? Well, first of all, if you loved mercy that much, you'd be constantly looking for opportunities to practice it, to show it to others. You would rejoice every time you were able to demonstrate mercy.

Second, you would automatically become less critical and judgmental. James wrote, "For he shall have judgment without mercy, that hath shewed no mercy; and mercy rejoiceth against judgment" (James 2:13). When someone is about to be judged and harshly punished for a wrong but is instead pardoned, you would *rejoice* that mercy prevailed over judgment.

Third, you yourself would be pardoned by God for your many sins and blunders, because Jesus said, "Forgive, and ye shall be forgiven" (Luke 6:37). And when God forgives you, His blessings can then begin to pour into your life. You can be certain of this, because Romans 4:7 says, "Blessed are they whose iniquities are forgiven, and whose sins are covered." So forgive others today!

He that covereth a transgression seeketh love; but he that repeateth a matter separateth very friends.

PROVERBS 17:9

∽

With the merciful thou wilt shew thyself merciful.

PSALM 18:25

∽

He hath shewed thee, O man, what is good; and what doth the LORD require of thee, but to do justly, and to love mercy, and to walk humbly with thy God?

MICAH 6:8

∽

Blessed are the merciful: for they shall obtain mercy.

MATTHEW 5:7

∽

For if ye forgive men their trespasses, your heavenly Father will also forgive you: but if ye forgive not men their trespasses, neither will your Father forgive your trespasses.

MATTHEW 6:14–15

∽

Then came Peter to him, and said, Lord, how oft shall my brother sin against me, and I forgive him? till seven times? Jesus saith unto him, I say not unto thee, Until seven times: but, Until seventy times seven.

MATTHEW 18:21–22

∽

For he shall have judgment without mercy, that hath shewed no mercy; and mercy rejoiceth against judgment.

JAMES 2:13

Therefore is the kingdom of heaven likened unto a certain king, which would take account of his servants. And when he had begun to reckon, one was brought unto him, which owed him ten thousand talents. But forasmuch as he had not to pay, his lord commanded him to be sold, and his wife, and children, and all that he had, and payment to be made. The servant therefore fell down, and worshipped him, saying, Lord, have patience with me, and I will pay thee all. Then the lord of that servant was moved with compassion, and loosed him, and forgave him the debt. But the same servant went out, and found one of his fellowservants, which owed him an hundred pence: and he laid hands on him, and took him by the throat, saying, Pay me that thou owest. And his fellowservant fell down at his feet, and besought him, saying, Have patience with me, and I will pay thee all. And he would not: but went and cast him into prison, till he should pay the debt. So when his fellowservants saw what was done, they were very sorry, and came and told unto their lord all that was done. Then his lord, after that he had called him, said unto him, O thou wicked servant, I forgave thee all that debt, because thou desiredst me: shouldest not thou also have had compassion on thy fellowservant, even as I had pity on thee? And his lord was wroth, and delivered him to the tormentors, till he should pay all that was due unto him. So likewise shall my heavenly Father do also unto you, if ye from your hearts forgive not every one his brother their trespasses.

MATTHEW 18:23–35

Judge not, and ye shall not be judged: condemn not, and ye shall not be condemned: forgive, and ye shall be forgiven.

LUKE 6:37

And when ye stand praying, forgive, if ye have ought against any: that your Father also which is in heaven may forgive you your trespasses.

MARK 11:25

And be ye kind one to another, tenderhearted, forgiving one another, even as God for Christ's sake hath forgiven you.

EPHESIANS 4:32

Forbearing one another, and forgiving one another, if any man have a quarrel against any: even as Christ forgave you, so also do ye.

COLOSSIANS 3:13

34. FELLOWSHIP AND UNITY

Psalm 133:1 says, "Behold, how good and how pleasant it is for brethren to dwell together in unity!" Some Christians, however, noting that disagreements are often a problem in the church, see this as a lofty ideal, something to strive for, but with little hope of attaining it in this life. But Jesus prayed "that [we] may be made perfect in one" (John 17:23), so He obviously expected Christians to experience a large measure of unity.

Some Christian groups think unity means conformity. Paul wrote, "I beseech you. . .that ye all speak the same thing, and that there be no divisions among you" (1 Corinthians 1:10), so they require their members to speak "the same thing" by having them memorize the same doctrines and Bible verses. They literally "say the same thing," word for word, like a tape-recorded message.

True unity, however, is an outworking of the Holy Spirit who dwells within you. Paul said the only way for there to be "no schism in the body" is if all the members "have the same care one for another" (1 Corinthians 12:25). When you love others and care for them, then instead of pushing to get your own way or bulldozing over them, you consider *their* needs, wishes, and concerns and act accordingly.

If you love others, you'll strive to be in unity with them.

So all the men of Israel were gathered against the city, knit together as one man.

JUDGES 20:11

Behold, how good and how pleasant it is for brethren to dwell together in unity!

PSALM 133:1

Two are better than one; because they have a good reward for their labour. For if they fall, the one will lift up his fellow: but woe to him that is alone when he falleth; for he hath not another to help him up. Again, if two lie together, then they have heat: but how can one be warm alone? And if one prevail against him, two shall withstand him; and a threefold cord is not quickly broken.

ECCLESIASTES 4:9–12

Again I say unto you, That if two of you shall agree on earth as touching any thing that they shall ask, it shall be done for them of my Father which is in heaven. For where two or three are gathered together in my name, there am I in the midst of them.

MATTHEW 18:19–20

Now I beseech you, brethren, by the name of our Lord Jesus Christ, that ye all speak the same thing, and that there be no divisions among you; but that ye be perfectly joined together in the same mind and in the same judgment.

1 CORINTHIANS 1:10

That they all may be one; as thou, Father, art in me, and I in thee, that they also may be one in us: that the world may believe that thou hast sent me. And the glory which thou gavest me I have given them; that they may be one, even as we are one: I in them, and thou in me, that they may be made perfect in one.

JOHN 17:21–23

So we, being many, are one body in Christ, and every one members one of another.

ROMANS 12:5

Let us therefore follow after the things which make for peace, and things wherewith one may edify another.

ROMANS 14:19

Now the God of patience and consolation grant you to be likeminded one toward another according to Christ Jesus: that ye may with one mind and one mouth glorify God, even the Father of our Lord Jesus Christ.

ROMANS 15:5–6

That there should be no schism in the body; but that the members should have the same care one for another. And whether one member suffer, all the members suffer with it; or one member be honoured, all the members rejoice with it. Now ye are the body of Christ, and members in particular.

1 CORINTHIANS 12:25–27

Be perfect, be of good comfort, be of one mind, live in peace; and the God of love and peace shall be with you.

2 CORINTHIANS 13:11

∞

Fulfil ye my joy, that ye be likeminded, having the same love, being of one accord, of one mind.

PHILIPPIANS 2:2

∞

And let the peace of God rule in your hearts, to the which also ye are called in one body; and be ye thankful.

COLOSSIANS 3:15

∞

Endeavouring to keep the unity of the Spirit in the bond of peace.

EPHESIANS 4:3

∞

From whom the whole body fitly joined together and compacted by that which every joint supplieth, according to the effectual working in the measure of every part, maketh increase of the body unto the edifying of itself in love.

EPHESIANS 4:16

35. SERVING AND HELPING OTHERS

The Israelite prophets repeatedly hammered home a message of social justice, of fairness, and of willingness to help your neighbor. This topic is extremely important to God.

Proverbs 14:21 says, "He that hath mercy on the poor, happy is he." This doesn't just mean giving them money. It also means giving of your time and putting forth the effort to show the lonely and the needy love in practical ways.

In one parable, Jesus spoke of a king whose subjects had unselfishly helped the poor. The king told them, "Inasmuch as ye have done it unto one of the least of these my brethren, ye have done it unto me" (Matthew 25:40). Reaching out to the weak, the oppressed, and the marginalized is an integral part of being Jesus' disciple.

Jesus often spoke of becoming a servant to others, but this is a difficult concept for many modern Christians. Many in the West seek "the abundant life" and proclaim that "nothing is too good for God's children." The emphasis is largely on self and on what God can do for them.

But the Bible teaches, "In lowliness of mind let each esteem other better than themselves" (Philippians 2:3). Only when you really believe in living this way will you be willing to become a "servant of all" (Mark 9:35).

And when ye reap the harvest of your land, thou shalt not wholly reap the corners of thy field, neither shalt thou gather the gleanings of thy harvest. And thou shalt not glean thy vineyard, neither shalt thou gather every grape of thy vineyard; thou shalt leave them for the poor and stranger: I am the LORD your God.

LEVITICUS 19:9–10

∞

Even as the Son of man came not to be ministered unto, but to minister.

MATTHEW 20:28

∞

But he that is greatest among you shall be your servant.

MATTHEW 23:11

∞

Then shall the King say unto them on his right hand, Come, ye blessed of my Father, inherit the kingdom prepared for you from the foundation of the world: for I was an hungred, and ye gave me meat: I was thirsty, and ye gave me drink: I was a stranger, and ye took me in: naked, and ye clothed me: I was sick, and ye visited me: I was in prison, and ye came unto me. Then shall the righteous answer him, saying, Lord, when saw we thee an hungred, and fed thee? or thirsty, and gave thee drink? When saw we thee a stranger, and took thee in? or naked, and clothed thee? Or when saw we thee sick, or in prison, and came unto thee? And the King shall answer and say unto them, Verily I say unto you, Inasmuch as ye have done it unto one of the least of these my brethren, ye have done it unto me.

MATTHEW 25:34–40

*And he sat down, and called the twelve, and saith unto
them, If any man desire to be first, the same shall be last of
all, and servant of all.*

MARK 9:35

*He that hath two coats, let him impart to him that hath
none; and he that hath meat, let him do likewise.*

LUKE 3:11

*A certain man went down from Jerusalem to Jericho, and
fell among thieves, which stripped him of his raiment, and
wounded him, and departed, leaving him half dead. . . .
But a certain Samaritan, as he journeyed, came where he
was: and when he saw him, he had compassion on him,
and went to him, and bound up his wounds, pouring in oil
and wine, and set him on his own beast, and brought him
to an inn, and took care of him. And on the morrow when
he departed, he took out two pence, and gave them to the
host, and said unto him, Take care of him; and whatsoever
thou spendest more, when I come again, I will repay thee.*

LUKE 10:30, 33–35

*If a brother or sister be naked, and destitute of daily food,
and one of you say unto them, Depart in peace, be ye
warmed and filled; notwithstanding ye give them not those
things which are needful to the body; what doth it profit?*

JAMES 2:15–16

As we have therefore opportunity, let us do good unto all men, especially unto them who are of the household of faith.

GALATIANS 6:10

But whoso hath this world's good, and seeth his brother have need, and shutteth up his bowels of compassion from him, how dwelleth the love of God in him? My little children, let us not love in word, neither in tongue; but in deed and in truth.

1 JOHN 3:17–18

36. GIVING TO OTHERS

Many Christians are surprised at how often the Bible speaks of giving money to the poor. The Hebrew prophets repeatedly spoke of this, and Jesus Himself brought it up time and time again. But some people ask, "Didn't Paul say, 'This we commanded you, that if any would not work, neither should he eat'?" (2 Thessalonians 3:10). Based on that one isolated verse, they then ignore all the words of the prophets and even Christ's repeated commands to help the poor.

People *are* to work to earn a living, but many people these days can't find work that pays a living wage. Or they're unable to find work at all. They're like the men whom a landowner found standing in the marketplace. When he asked them, "Why stand ye here all the day idle?" they answered, "Because no man hath hired us" (Matthew 20:6–7). Many people aren't always poor. They just need help to make it through a difficult time.

If you can't afford to give money, at least consider lending them money to help them through a tight spot. The Bible commands, "Thou shalt open thine hand wide unto thy brother, to thy poor, and to thy needy, in thy land" (Deuteronomy 15:11). And God promised that if you obey Him in this, He will bless you.

If there be among you a poor man of one of thy brethren within any of thy gates in thy land which the LORD thy God giveth thee, thou shalt not harden thine heart, nor shut thine hand from thy poor brother: but thou shalt open thine hand wide unto him, and shalt surely lend him sufficient for his need, in that which he wanteth. Beware that there be not a thought in thy wicked heart, saying, The seventh year, the year of release, is at hand; and thine eye be evil against thy poor brother, and thou givest him nought; and he cry unto the LORD against thee, and it be sin unto thee. Thou shalt surely give him, and thine heart shall not be grieved when thou givest unto him: because that for this thing the LORD thy God shall bless thee in all thy works, and in all that thou puttest thine hand unto. For the poor shall never cease out of the land: therefore I command thee, saying, Thou shalt open thine hand wide unto thy brother, to thy poor, and to thy needy, in thy land.

DEUTERONOMY 15:7–11

Withhold not good from them to whom it is due, when it is in the power of thine hand to do it.

PROVERBS 3:27

He that hath pity upon the poor lendeth unto the LORD; and that which he hath given will he pay him again.

PROVERBS 19:17

He that hath a bountiful eye shall be blessed; for he giveth of his bread to the poor.

PROVERBS 22:9

He that giveth unto the poor shall not lack: but he that hideth his eyes shall have many a curse.

PROVERBS 28:27

∞

Give to him that asketh thee, and from him that would borrow of thee turn not thou away.

MATTHEW 5:42

∞

One thing thou lackest: go thy way, sell whatsoever thou hast, and give to the poor, and thou shalt have treasure in heaven.

MARK 10:21

∞

Give, and it shall be given unto you; good measure, pressed down, and shaken together, and running over, shall men give into your bosom.

LUKE 6:38

∞

And all that believed were together, and had all things common; and sold their possessions and goods, and parted them to all men, as every man had need.

ACTS 2:44–45

∞

Now ye Philippians know also, that in the beginning of the gospel, when I departed from Macedonia, no church communicated with me as concerning giving and receiving, but ye only. For even in Thessalonica ye sent once and again unto my necessity.

PHILIPPIANS 4:15–16

And the multitude of them that believed were of one heart and of one soul: neither said any of them that ought of the things which he possessed was his own; but they had all things common. . . . Neither was there any among them that lacked: for as many as were possessors of lands or houses sold them, and brought the prices of the things that were sold, and laid them down at the apostles' feet: and distribution was made unto every man according as he had need.

ACTS 4:32, 34–35

∽

For it hath pleased them of Macedonia and Achaia to make a certain contribution for the poor saints which are at Jerusalem.

ROMANS 15:26

∽

Distributing to the necessity of saints; given to hospitality.

ROMANS 12:13

∽

Only they would that we should remember the poor; the same which I also was forward to do.

GALATIANS 2:10

37. WITNESSING FOR CHRIST

Christians commonly use the word *witnessing* to refer to "preaching the Gospel" or telling others how Jesus can save them. According to the dictionary, a *witness* is "a person who sees an event happening, especially a crime or an accident." The apostles and other early Christians witnessed Jesus' death and resurrection, so God called upon them to "be witnesses" to these facts, to "bear witness" to the truth. Jesus told His first disciples, "Ye shall be witnesses unto me. . .unto the uttermost part of the earth" (Acts 1:8; see also 2:32; 3:15; 5:32; 10:39).

Although you didn't watch Jesus die on the cross or see Him after He rose from the dead, you can bear witness to the changes He has made in your life. You can still preach the Gospel of salvation. In fact, God is counting on you to help share the Good News. Jesus said, "Go ye into all the world, and preach the gospel to every creature" (Mark 16:15)—and this task isn't complete yet, so you must help finish the job. Only after the Gospel is preached in all the world can Jesus return.

You're probably not a bold evangelist, and perhaps you've even had difficulty evangelizing your friends and family. But pray for opportunities to be a witness— both by your words and by your example. And support missionaries who preach the Gospel full-time.

*Let your light so shine before men, that they may see your
good works, and glorify your Father which is in heaven.*

MATTHEW 5:16

∞

*Then saith he unto his disciples, The harvest truly is
plenteous, but the labourers are few; pray ye therefore
the Lord of the harvest, that he will send forth labourers
into his harvest.*

MATTHEW 9:37–38

∞

*Go ye therefore, and teach all nations, baptizing them in
the name of the Father, and of the Son, and of the Holy
Ghost: teaching them to observe all things whatsoever I
have commanded you.*

MATTHEW 28:19–20

∞

And the gospel must first be published among all nations.

MARK 13:10

∞

*Go ye into all the world, and preach the gospel to every
creature.*

MARK 16:15

∞

*Thus it is written, and thus it behooved Christ to suffer,
and to rise from the dead the third day: and that
repentance and remission of sins should be preached in his
name among all nations, beginning at Jerusalem. And ye
are witnesses of these things.*

LUKE 24:46–48

But ye shall receive power, after that the Holy Ghost is come upon you: and ye shall be witnesses unto me both in Jerusalem, and in all Judaea, and in Samaria, and unto the uttermost part of the earth.

ACTS 1:8

∞

And they were all filled with the Holy Ghost, and they spake the word of God with boldness.

ACTS 4:31

∞

And daily in the temple, and in every house, they ceased not to teach and preach Jesus Christ.

ACTS 5:42

∞

For he mightily convinced the Jews, and that publicly, shewing by the scriptures that Jesus was Christ.

ACTS 18:28

∞

To open their eyes, and to turn them from darkness to light, and from the power of Satan unto God, that they may receive forgiveness of sins, and inheritance among them which are sanctified by faith that is in me.

ACTS 26:18

∞

For I am not ashamed of the gospel of Christ: for it is the power of God unto salvation to every one that believeth.

ROMANS 1:16

How then shall they call on him in whom they have not believed? and how shall they believe in him of whom they have not heard? and how shall they hear without a preacher? and how shall they preach, except they be sent? as it is written, How beautiful are the feet of them that preach the gospel of peace, and bring glad tidings of good things!

ROMANS 10:14–15

∞

For though I preach the gospel, I have nothing to glory of: for necessity is laid upon me; yea, woe is unto me, if I preach not the gospel! For if I do this thing willingly, I have a reward: but if against my will, a dispensation of the gospel is committed unto me.

1 CORINTHIANS 9:16–17

∞

Now then we are ambassadors for Christ, as though God did beseech you by us: we pray you in Christ's stead, be ye reconciled to God.

2 CORINTHIANS 5:20

∞

Let him know, that he which converteth the sinner from the error of his way shall save a soul from death, and shall hide a multitude of sins.

JAMES 5:20

∞

But sanctify the Lord God in your hearts: and be ready always to give an answer to every man that asketh you a reason of the hope that is in you with meekness and fear.

1 PETER 3:15

38. ENDURING PERSECUTION

Persecution for Christ ranges from mild disapproval to torture, from being excluded from certain social groups to being martyred. Jesus said, "They shall put you out of the synagogues: yea, the time cometh, that whosoever killeth you will think that he doeth God service" (John 16:2).

Most of the persecution you're likely to face in North America will consist of verbal abuse. As Jesus said, "Men shall revile you. . .and shall say all manner of evil against you falsely" (Matthew 5:11).

You should *expect* persecution. Then, when "tribulation or persecution ariseth because of the word" (Matthew 13:21), you won't be offended. Peter said persecution isn't a strange thing for a follower of Christ. It's normal. "Beloved, think it not strange concerning the fiery trial which is to try you, as though some strange thing happened unto you: but rejoice, inasmuch as ye are partakers of Christ's sufferings" (1 Peter 4:12–13).

Paul warned, "For unto you it is given in the behalf of Christ, not only to believe on him, but also to suffer for his sake" (Philippians 1:29). But remember, when you're suffering, you're partaking of *Christ's* sufferings. Jesus Himself was slandered. He suffered rejection, physical beatings, torture, and even death—and He promised that if people treated *Him* that way, then His followers could expect the same (John 15:20).

Many are my persecutors and mine enemies; yet do I not decline from thy testimonies.

PSALM 119:157

Blessed are they which are persecuted for righteousness' sake: for theirs is the kingdom of heaven. Blessed are ye, when men shall revile you, and persecute you, and shall say all manner of evil against you falsely, for my sake. Rejoice, and be exceeding glad: for great is your reward in heaven: for so persecuted they the prophets which were before you.

MATTHEW 5:10–12

But beware of men: for they will deliver you up to the councils, and they will scourge you in their synagogues; and ye shall be brought before governors and kings for my sake.

MATTHEW 10:17–18

Then shall they deliver you up to be afflicted, and shall kill you: and ye shall be hated of all nations for my name's sake. And then shall many be offended, and shall betray one another, and shall hate one another.

MATTHEW 24:9–10

Remember the word that I said unto you, The servant is not greater than his lord. If they have persecuted me, they will also persecute you; if they have kept my saying, they will keep yours also.

JOHN 15:20

These things I have spoken unto you, that in me ye might have peace. In the world ye shall have tribulation: but be of good cheer; I have overcome the world.

JOHN 16:33

∽

And if children, then heirs; heirs of God, and joint-heirs with Christ; if so be that we suffer with him, that we may be also glorified together. For I reckon that the sufferings of this present time are not worthy to be compared with the glory which shall be revealed in us.

ROMANS 8:17–18

∽

We are troubled on every side, yet not distressed; we are perplexed, but not in despair; persecuted, but not forsaken; cast down, but not destroyed; always bearing about in the body the dying of the Lord Jesus, that the life also of Jesus might be made manifest in our body.

2 CORINTHIANS 4:8–10

∽

Therefore I take pleasure. . .in persecutions, in distresses for Christ's sake: for when I am weak, then am I strong.

2 CORINTHIANS 12:10

∽

For unto you it is given in the behalf of Christ, not only to believe on him, but also to suffer for his sake.

PHILIPPIANS 1:29

That no man should be moved by these afflictions: for yourselves know that we are appointed thereunto.

1 THESSALONIANS 3:3

❀

So that we ourselves glory in you in the churches of God for your patience and faith in all your persecutions and tribulations that ye endure.

2 THESSALONIANS 1:4

❀

If we suffer, we shall also reign with him: if we deny him, he also will deny us.

2 TIMOTHY 2:12

❀

By faith Moses, when he was come to years, refused to be called the son of Pharaoh's daughter; choosing rather to suffer affliction with the people of God, than to enjoy the pleasures of sin for a season; esteeming the reproach of Christ greater riches than the treasures in Egypt: for he had respect unto the recompence of the reward.

HEBREWS 11:24–26

❀

Beloved, think it not strange concerning the fiery trial which is to try you, as though some strange thing happened unto you: but rejoice, inasmuch as ye are partakers of Christ's sufferings; that, when his glory shall be revealed, ye may be glad also with exceeding joy.

1 PETER 4:12–13

39. COMPROMISING

The word *compromise* can have a positive meaning. For example, when two groups both have entrenched positions, it's beneficial if they're willing to compromise certain details in the interest of reaching a peaceful agreement. But when it comes to spiritual matters, compromise has negative connotations. It means to not live up to the truth you know, to do something wrong that weakens you spiritually.

Often people compromise with others because they like them, owe them favors, or are afraid of them. Saul is a classic example. God told him to wipe out all the wicked Amalekites and their possessions, but after defeating them, Saul allowed the Israelites to keep the healthy animals from their flocks and herds. When the prophet Samuel confronted Saul about this, Saul said, "I have sinned: for I have transgressed the commandment of the LORD, and thy words: because I feared the people, and obeyed their voice" (1 Samuel 15:24).

After Samuel reproved Saul for compromising and told him he would lose the throne over it, Saul said, "I have sinned: yet honour me now, I pray thee, before the elders of my people, and before Israel" (15:30). Even as he went down, Saul was still seeking to put on a show for the benefit of the people.

And thou shalt take no gift: for the gift blindeth the wise, and perverteth the words of the righteous.

EXODUS 23:8

∞

Thou shalt make no covenant with them, nor with their gods. They shall not dwell in thy land, lest they make thee sin against me: for if thou serve their gods, it will surely be a snare unto thee.

EXODUS 23:32–33

∞

And Balaam answered and said unto the servants of Balak, If Balak would give me his house full of silver and gold, I cannot go beyond the word of the LORD my God, to do less or more.

NUMBERS 22:18

∞

And ye shall make no league with the inhabitants of this land; ye shall throw down their altars: but ye have not obeyed my voice: why have ye done this? Wherefore I also said, I will not drive them out from before you; but they shall be as thorns in your sides, and their gods shall be a snare unto you.

JUDGES 2:2–3

∞

And the children of Israel dwelt among the Canaanites. . . and they took their daughters to be their wives, and gave their daughters to their sons, and served their gods.

JUDGES 3:5–6

*Of the nations concerning which the LORD said unto the
children of Israel, Ye shall not go in to them, neither shall
they come in unto you: for surely they will turn away your
heart after their gods: Solomon clave unto these in love.
And he had seven hundred wives, princesses, and three
hundred concubines: and his wives turned away his heart.*

1 KINGS 11:2–3

∞

*How long halt ye between two opinions? if the LORD be
God, follow him: but if Baal, then follow him. And the
people answered him not a word.*

1 KINGS 18:21

∞

*And Naaman said. . .Thy servant will henceforth offer
neither burnt offering nor sacrifice unto other gods, but
unto the LORD. In this thing the LORD pardon thy servant,
that when my master goeth into the house of Rimmon
to worship there, and he leaneth on my hand, and I bow
myself in the house of Rimmon: when I bow down myself
in the house of Rimmon, the LORD pardon thy servant in
this thing.*

2 KINGS 5:17–18

∞

*These words spake his parents, because they feared the
Jews: for the Jews had agreed already, that if any man
did confess that he was Christ, he should be put out of the
synagogue.*

JOHN 9:22

Nevertheless among the chief rulers also many believed on him; but because of the Pharisees they did not confess him, lest they should be put out of the synagogue: for they loved the praise of men more than the praise of God.

JOHN 12:42–43

∞

Be ye not unequally yoked together with unbelievers: for what fellowship hath righteousness with unrighteousness? and what communion hath light with darkness? And what concord hath Christ with Belial? or what part hath he that believeth with an infidel? And what agreement hath the temple of God with idols? . . . Wherefore come out from among them, and be ye separate, saith the Lord, and touch not the unclean thing; and I will receive you.

2 CORINTHIANS 6:14–17

∞

The fear of man bringeth a snare.

PROVERBS 29:25

∞

As many as desire to make a fair shew in the flesh, they constrain you to be circumcised; only lest they should suffer persecution for the cross of Christ.

GALATIANS 6:12

40. DYING TO SELF

Jesus spoke quite a bit about "dying to self" and "forsaking all," and it's not the part of His teachings that Christians are most enthusiastic about. Nor are they happy with Paul's expression "crucified with Christ." They'd much rather focus on God's love and forgiveness, or on His many blessings.

But Jesus made it clear that it's in dying to self that you find true life, and in giving up your goals and rights and desires that you truly experience being His disciple. It may seem paradoxical, but as Jesus explained, a kernel of wheat can't bring forth new life unless it "dies" by being buried in the soil. Thus He said, "He that loveth his life shall lose it; and he that hateth his life in this world shall keep it unto life eternal" (John 12:24–25).

Except for moments when you're down and discouraged, "hating your life" doesn't come naturally. As Paul declared, "For no man ever yet hated his own flesh; but nourisheth and cherisheth it" (Ephesians 5:29). But when you're motivated by God's love, you become willing to stop putting yourself first and to live your life for God and others, instead of for selfish pleasure or gain. "Greater love hath no man than this, that a man lay down his life for his friends" (John 15:13).

And Jesus answered and said, Verily I say unto you, There is no man that hath left house, or brethren, or sisters, or father, or mother, or wife, or children, or lands, for my sake, and the gospel's, but he shall receive an hundredfold now in this time. . .with persecutions; and in the world to come eternal life.

MARK 10:29–30

And it came to pass, that, as they went in the way, a certain man said unto him, Lord, I will follow thee whithersoever thou goest. And Jesus said unto him, Foxes have holes, and birds of the air have nests; but the Son of man hath not where to lay his head.

LUKE 9:57–58

And he said unto another, Follow me. But he said, Lord, suffer me first to go and bury my father. Jesus said unto him, Let the dead bury their dead: but go thou and preach the kingdom of God.

LUKE 9:59–60

And another also said, Lord, I will follow thee; but let me first go bid them farewell, which are at home at my house. And Jesus said unto him, No man, having put his hand to the plough, and looking back, is fit for the kingdom of God.

LUKE 9:61–62

Greater love hath no man than this, that a man lay down his life for his friends.

JOHN 15:13

If any man come to me, and hate not his father, and mother, and wife, and children, and brethren, and sisters, yea, and his own life also, he cannot be my disciple. And whosoever doth not bear his cross, and come after me, cannot be my disciple.

LUKE 14:26–27

∞

For which of you, intending to build a tower, sitteth not down first, and counteth the cost, whether he have sufficient to finish it? Lest haply, after he hath laid the foundation, and is not able to finish it, all that behold it begin to mock him, saying, This man began to build, and was not able to finish. Or what king, going to make war against another king, sitteth not down first, and consulteth whether he be able with ten thousand to meet him that cometh against him with twenty thousand? Or else, while the other is yet a great way off, he sendeth an ambassage, and desireth conditions of peace. So likewise, whosoever he be of you that forsaketh not all that he hath, he cannot be my disciple.

LUKE 14:28–33

∞

Except a corn of wheat fall into the ground and die, it abideth alone: but if it die, it bringeth forth much fruit. He that loveth his life shall lose it; and he that hateth his life in this world shall keep it unto life eternal.

JOHN 12:24–25

∞

If any man serve me, let him follow me; and where I am, there shall also my servant be: if any man serve me, him will my Father honour.

JOHN 12:26

I beseech you therefore, brethren, by the mercies of God, that ye present your bodies a living sacrifice, holy, acceptable unto God, which is your reasonable service.

ROMANS 12:1

I am crucified with Christ: nevertheless I live; yet not I, but Christ liveth in me: and the life which I now live in the flesh I live by the faith of the Son of God, who loved me, and gave himself for me.

GALATIANS 2:20

41. BACKSLIDING

A backslider is someone who once had faith in Christ and was following the Lord, but then looked back longingly at their old life and eventually returned to their sinful ways. Jeremiah 17:5 speaks of "the man. . .whose heart departeth from the LORD." Backsliders think about turning back long before they actually physically do so, which is why Proverbs 14:14 says, "The backslider in heart shall be filled with his own ways."

"And truly, if they had been mindful of that country from whence they came out, they might have had opportunity to have returned" (Hebrews 11:15). If your mind is becoming full of the world again, you'll start seeking ways to return to your former lifestyle. Jesus warned, "No man, having put his hand to the plough, and looking back, is fit for the kingdom of God" (Luke 9:62). It's that longing look back that does you in.

Solomon confessed, "I was almost in all evil in the midst of the congregation and assembly" (Proverbs 5:14). Many people still attend church and go through the motions of living a Christian life but are backslidden in heart, involved in compromise and sin.

The Bible doesn't have very complimentary things to say about backsliding. It declares, "As a dog returneth to his vomit, so a fool returneth to his folly" (Proverbs 26:11).

But his wife looked back from behind him, and she became a pillar of salt.

GENESIS 19:26

But as for me, my feet were almost gone; my steps had well nigh slipped. For I was envious at the foolish, when I saw the prosperity of the wicked.

PSALM 73:2–3

Ye have said, It is vain to serve God: and what profit is it that we have kept his ordinance?

MALACHI 3:14

And every one that heareth these sayings of mine, and doeth them not, shall be likened unto a foolish man, which built his house upon the sand: and the rain descended, and the floods came, and the winds blew, and beat upon that house; and it fell: and great was the fall of it.

MATTHEW 7:26–27

But he that received the seed into stony places, the same is he that heareth the word, and anon with joy receiveth it; yet hath he not root in himself, but dureth for a while: for when tribulation or persecution ariseth because of the word, by and by he is offended. He also that received seed among the thorns is he that heareth the word; and the care of this world, and the deceitfulness of riches, choke the word, and he becometh unfruitful.

MATTHEW 13:20–22

*This people draweth nigh unto me with their mouth, and
honoureth me with their lips; but their heart is far from me.*

MATTHEW 15:8

∞

*They on the rock are they, which, when they hear, receive
the word with joy; and these have no root, which for a
while believe, and in time of temptation fall away.*

LUKE 8:13

∞

*Many therefore of his disciples, when they had heard this,
said, This is an hard saying; who can hear it? . . . From
that time many of his disciples went back, and walked no
more with him.*

JOHN 6:60, 66

∞

*Beware lest any man spoil you through philosophy and
vain deceit, after the tradition of men, after the rudiments
of the world, and not after Christ.*

COLOSSIANS 2:8

∞

*Take heed, brethren, lest there be in any of you an evil
heart of unbelief, in departing from the living God.*

HEBREWS 3:12

∞

*Lest there be any fornicator, or profane person, as Esau,
who for one morsel of meat sold his birthright.*

HEBREWS 12:16

But it is happened unto them according to the true proverb, The dog is turned to his own vomit again; and the sow that was washed to her wallowing in the mire.

2 PETER 2:22

Holding faith, and a good conscience; which some having put away concerning faith have made shipwreck.

1 TIMOTHY 1:19

But they that will be rich fall into temptation and a snare, and into many foolish and hurtful lusts, which drown men in destruction and perdition.

1 TIMOTHY 6:9

Love not the world, neither the things that are in the world. If any man love the world, the love of the Father is not in him.

1 JOHN 2:15

I have somewhat against thee, because thou hast left thy first love. Remember therefore from whence thou art fallen, and repent, and do the first works.

REVELATION 2:4–5

I know thy works, that thou art neither cold nor hot: I would thou wert cold or hot. So then because thou art lukewarm, and neither cold nor hot, I will spue thee out of my mouth.

REVELATION 3:15–16

42. REPENTANCE

The Greek words *metanoia* and *metamelomai*, translated "repent" and "repentance" in the New Testament, mean "a transforming change of heart; especially a spiritual conversion."

When repenting of their sins, the Jews of the Old Testament would frequently rip their fine garments, dress in coarse material called "sackcloth," smear ashes on their faces, and pour dust on their heads. They would also publicly weep, lay sprawled in the dust, and fast from food. They did these things to show that they were greatly abasing themselves before God.

But like many religious observances, sometimes these actions degenerated into a mere show. So God said, "Turn ye even to me with *all your heart*, and with fasting, and with weeping, and with mourning: and *rend your heart*, and not your garments" (Joel 2:12–13, emphasis added).

In Isaiah 58:5–6, God asked, "Is it such a fast that I have chosen? a day for a man to afflict his soul? is it to bow down his head. . .and to spread sackcloth and ashes under him?" He then answered His question, saying, "Is not this the fast that I have chosen? to loose the bands of wickedness, to undo the heavy burdens, and to let the oppressed go free?" God looks for real repentance and a genuine change of heart. Paul said to "do works meet for [in keeping with] repentance" (Acts 26:20).

And the LORD shall scatter you among the nations, and ye shall be left few in number among the heathen. . . . But if from thence thou shalt seek the LORD thy God, thou shalt find him, if thou seek him with all thy heart and with all thy soul.

DEUTERONOMY 4:27, 29

But Hezekiah rendered not again according to the benefit done unto him; for his heart was lifted up: therefore there was wrath upon him, and upon Judah and Jerusalem. Notwithstanding Hezekiah humbled himself for the pride of his heart, both he and the inhabitants of Jerusalem, so that the wrath of the LORD came not upon them in the days of Hezekiah.

2 CHRONICLES 32:25–26

All the paths of the LORD are mercy and truth unto such as keep his covenant and his testimonies.

PSALM 25:10

When wisdom entereth into thine heart, and knowledge is pleasant unto thy soul; discretion shall preserve thee, understanding shall keep thee: to deliver thee from the way of the evil man, from the man that speaketh froward things; who leave the paths of uprightness, to walk in the ways of darkness.

PROVERBS 2:10–13

Wherefore I abhor myself, and repent in dust and ashes.

JOB 42:6

I hearkened and heard, but they spake not aright: no man repented him of his wickedness, saying, What have I done? every one turned to his course, as the horse rusheth into the battle.

JEREMIAH 8:6

Repent, and turn yourselves from all your transgressions; so iniquity shall not be your ruin.

EZEKIEL 18:30

O Israel, return unto the LORD thy God; for thou hast fallen by thine iniquity. Take with you words, and turn to the LORD: say unto him, Take away all iniquity, and receive us graciously: so will we render the calves of our lips. . . . I will heal their backsliding, I will love them freely: for mine anger is turned away from him.

HOSEA 14:1–2, 4

Therefore also now, saith the LORD, turn ye even to me with all your heart, and with fasting, and with weeping, and with mourning: and rend your heart, and not your garments, and turn unto the LORD your God: for he is gracious and merciful, slow to anger, and of great kindness, and repenteth him of the evil.

JOEL 2:12–13

Bring forth therefore fruits meet for repentance.

MATTHEW 3:8

∽

*From that time Jesus began to preach, and to say, Repent:
for the kingdom of heaven is at hand.*

MATTHEW 4:17

∽

*Likewise, I say unto you, there is joy in the presence of the
angels of God over one sinner that repenteth.*

LUKE 15:10

∽

*Repent ye therefore, and be converted, that your sins may
be blotted out.*

ACTS 3:19

∽

*But [I] shewed first unto them of Damascus, and at
Jerusalem, and throughout all the coasts of Judaea, and
then to the Gentiles, that they should repent and turn to
God, and do works meet for repentance.*

ACTS 26:20

∽

*Or despisest thou the riches of his goodness and forbearance
and longsuffering; not knowing that the goodness of God
leadeth thee to repentance?*

ROMANS 2:4

43. GUILT AND CONDEMNATION

Before you had faith in Christ, you were guilty and condemned like the rest of the world. But when you believed in Jesus, you were no longer under condemnation. Jesus said, "He that heareth my word. . .shall not come into condemnation; but is passed from death unto life" (John 5:24). And John 3:18 says, "He that believeth on him is not condemned." You were "justified freely by his grace" (Romans 3:24).

But that doesn't stop the enemy of your soul, the devil, from condemning you for your past sins and insisting that God hasn't (and can't) forgive you. But as Paul wrote, "Who shall lay any thing to the charge of God's elect? It is God that justifieth. Who is he that condemneth? It is Christ that died. . .who also maketh intercession for us" (Romans 8:33–34). Paul sums things up by saying, "There is therefore now no condemnation to them which are in Christ Jesus" (Romans 8:1).

The devil accuses believers, including you, before God day and night, but you have already been cleansed by the blood of the Lamb (Revelation 12:10–11). Jesus' blood paid the price for your sins. God doesn't listen to the devil's lies, so don't you listen to them either. Refuse to be discouraged when he tells you that you're worthless, no good, and condemned.

Then Satan answered the LORD, and said, Doth Job fear God for nought? Hast not thou made an hedge about him, and about his house, and about all that he hath on every side? thou hast blessed the work of his hands, and his substance is increased in the land. But put forth thine hand now, and touch all that he hath, and he will curse thee to thy face.

JOB 1:9–11

And Satan answered the LORD, and said, Skin for skin, yea, all that a man hath will he give for his life. But put forth thine hand now, and touch his bone and his flesh, and he will curse thee to thy face.

JOB 2:4–5

And he shewed me Joshua the high priest standing before the angel of the LORD, and Satan standing at his right hand to resist him. And the LORD said unto Satan, The LORD rebuke thee, O Satan; even the LORD that hath chosen Jerusalem rebuke thee: is not this a brand plucked out of the fire? Now Joshua was clothed with filthy garments, and stood before the angel. And he answered and spake unto those that stood before him, saying, Take away the filthy garments from him. And unto him he said, Behold, I have caused thine iniquity to pass from thee, and I will clothe thee with change of raiment.

ZECHARIAH 3:1–4

When Simon Peter saw it, he fell down at Jesus' knees, saying, Depart from me; for I am a sinful man, O Lord . . . . And Jesus said unto Simon, Fear not; from henceforth thou shalt catch men. And when they had brought their ships to land, they forsook all, and followed him.

LUKE 5:8, 10–11

∞

Verily, verily, I say unto you, He that heareth my word, and believeth on him that sent me, hath everlasting life, and shall not come into condemnation; but is passed from death unto life.

JOHN 5:24

∞

There is therefore now no condemnation to them which are in Christ Jesus, who walk not after the flesh, but after the Spirit.

ROMANS 8:1

∞

What shall we then say to these things? If God be for us, who can be against us? He that spared not his own Son, but delivered him up for us all, how shall he not with him also freely give us all things? Who shall lay any thing to the charge of God's elect? It is God that justifieth. Who is he that condemneth? It is Christ that died, yea rather, that is risen again, who is even at the right hand of God, who also maketh intercession for us.

ROMANS 8:31–34

∞

So that contrariwise ye ought rather to forgive him, and comfort him, lest perhaps such a one should be swallowed up with overmuch sorrow.

2 CORINTHIANS 2:7

For if our heart condemn us, God is greater than our heart, and knoweth all things. Beloved, if our heart condemn us not, then have we confidence toward God. And whatsoever we ask, we receive of him, because we keep his commandments, and do those things that are pleasing in his sight.

1 JOHN 3:20–22

Now is come salvation, and strength, and the kingdom of our God, and the power of his Christ: for the accuser of our brethren is cast down, which accused them before our God day and night. And they overcame him by the blood of the Lamb.

REVELATION 12:10–11

44. PRIDE VERSUS HUMILITY

It's a human tendency to think more highly of yourself than you ought to, to become proud over your beauty, your talents, your accomplishments, or your wealth. Many people believe that taking pride in yourself is a good thing. But just because pride is a natural attitude doesn't mean it's right. Many attitudes in people's hearts displease God. Jesus said, "Thefts. . .pride, foolishness: all these evil things come from within, and defile the man" (Mark 7:22–23).

The Bible uses different words to describe pride, calling it arrogance, being haughty, having a high look, being lifted up, vaunting yourself, and so on.

A proud attitude disconnects you from the Lord. The Bible says, "An high look, and a proud heart. . .is sin" (Proverbs 21:4). If you're proud, you think more highly of yourself than you ought. You believe you can do things without God's help. Pride causes you to dis-connect from His power. That's why Psalm 138:6 says, "Though the LORD be high, yet hath he respect unto the lowly: but the proud he knoweth afar off."

God not only is distant from the arrogant but actually works against them. "God resisteth the proud, but giveth grace unto the humble" (James 4:6). Finally, the Bible warns, "A man's pride shall bring him low: but honour shall uphold the humble in spirit" (Proverbs 29:23).

And his name spread far abroad; for he was marvellously helped, till he was strong. But when he was strong, his heart was lifted up to his destruction: for he transgressed against the LORD.

2 CHRONICLES 26:15–16

∞

But Hezekiah rendered not again according to the benefit done unto him; for his heart was lifted up: therefore there was wrath upon him, and upon Judah and Jerusalem. Notwithstanding Hezekiah humbled himself for the pride of his heart, both he and the inhabitants of Jerusalem, so that the wrath of the LORD came not upon them in the days of Hezekiah.

2 CHRONICLES 32:25–26

∞

The wicked, through the pride of his countenance, will not seek after God: God is not in all his thoughts.

PSALM 10:4

∞

Though the LORD be high, yet hath he respect unto the lowly: but the proud he knoweth afar off.

PSALM 138:6

∞

These six things doth the LORD hate: yea, seven are an abomination unto him: a proud look. . .

PROVERBS 6:16–17

The fear of the LORD is to hate evil: pride, and arrogancy. . . do I hate.

PROVERBS 8:13

∞

When pride cometh, then cometh shame: but with the lowly is wisdom.

PROVERBS 11:2

∞

Only by pride cometh contention: but with the well advised is wisdom.

PROVERBS 13:10

∞

Every one that is proud in heart is an abomination to the LORD.

PROVERBS 16:5

∞

Pride goeth before destruction, and an haughty spirit before a fall.

PROVERBS 16:18

∞

Before destruction the heart of man is haughty, and before honour is humility.

PROVERBS 18:12

∞

Seest thou a man wise in his own conceit? there is more hope of a fool than of him.

PROVERBS 26:12

He that is of a proud heart stirreth up strife.

PROVERBS 28:25

❧

By thy great wisdom and by thy traffick hast thou increased thy riches, and thine heart is lifted up because of thy riches.

EZEKIEL 28:5

❧

Thine heart was lifted up because of thy beauty.

EZEKIEL 28:17

❧

The most high God gave Nebuchadnezzar thy father a kingdom, and majesty, and glory, and honour. . . . But when his heart was lifted up, and his mind hardened in pride, he was deposed from his kingly throne, and they took his glory from him.

DANIEL 5:18, 20

❧

The pride of thine heart hath deceived thee, thou that dwellest in the clefts of the rock, whose habitation is high; that saith in his heart, Who shall bring me down to the ground?

OBADIAH 1:3

❧

For I say, through the grace given unto me, to every man that is among you, not to think of himself more highly than he ought to think; but to think soberly.

ROMANS 12:3

45. SELF-RIGHTEOUSNESS AND HYPOCRISY

Christ's followers are to avoid being self-righteous. You do this by accepting that you can never be righteous enough to please God, and must depend on His righteousness. David wrote, "I will go in the strength of the Lord God: I make mention of *thy* righteousness, even of *thine only*" (Psalm 71:16, emphasis added).

Many scribes and Pharisees in Jesus' day, however, believed that they could become righteous by scrupulously obeying multitudes of legalistic religious rules. This thinking, however, was a deception and immediately created problems. First, they then thought they were superior to others, so they looked down on them and despised them (Luke 18:9–14).

Second, they felt that having contact with these "inferior" people contaminated them, so they separated themselves from them. (The name *Pharisee* means "set apart, separated.") If they brushed against a common Jew in the street, they would hurry home to wash. Isaiah described such people, saying, "Come not near to me; for I am holier than thou" (Isaiah 65:5). You can avoid having a sanctimonious attitude by obeying this command: "In lowliness of mind let each esteem other better than themselves" (Philippians 2:3).

You stumble into a self-righteous attitude when you lose touch with God's grace. So stay full of God's Spirit! Live a life overflowing with love. Then God's Holy Spirit in you will make you righteous.

There is a generation that are pure in their own eyes, and yet is not washed from their filthiness.

PROVERBS 30:12

∞

The scribes and the Pharisees sit in Moses' seat: all therefore whatsoever they bid you observe, that observe and do; but do not ye after their works: for they say, and do not. For they bind heavy burdens and grievous to be borne, and lay them on men's shoulders; but they themselves will not move them with one of their fingers.

MATTHEW 23:2–4

∞

Woe unto you, scribes and Pharisees, hypocrites! for ye devour widows' houses, and for a pretence make long prayer: therefore ye shall receive the greater damnation.

MATTHEW 23:14

∞

Woe unto you, scribes and Pharisees, hypocrites! for ye pay tithe of mint and anise and cummin, and have omitted the weightier matters of the law, judgment, mercy, and faith: these ought ye to have done, and not to leave the other undone. Ye blind guides, which strain at a gnat, and swallow a camel. Woe unto you, scribes and Pharisees, hypocrites! for ye make clean the outside of the cup and of the platter, but within they are full of extortion and excess. . . . Woe unto you, scribes and Pharisees, hypocrites! for ye are like unto whited sepulchres, which indeed appear beautiful outward, but are within full of dead men's bones, and of all uncleanness. Even so ye also outwardly appear righteous unto men, but within ye are full of hypocrisy and iniquity.

MATTHEW 23:23–25, 27–28

And why beholdest thou the mote that is in thy brother's eye, but perceivest not the beam that is in thine own eye? Either how canst thou say to thy brother, Brother, let me pull out the mote that is in thine eye, when thou thyself beholdest not the beam that is in thine own eye? Thou hypocrite, cast out first the beam out of thine own eye, and then shalt thou see clearly to pull out the mote that is in thy brother's eye.

LUKE 6:41–42

∽

And he spake this parable unto certain which trusted in themselves that they were righteous, and despised others: Two men went up into the temple to pray; the one a Pharisee, and the other a publican. The Pharisee stood and prayed thus with himself, God, I thank thee, that I am not as other men are, extortioners, unjust, adulterers, or even as this publican. I fast twice in the week, I give tithes of all that I possess. And the publican, standing afar off, would not lift up so much as his eyes unto heaven, but smote upon his breast, saying, God be merciful to me a sinner. I tell you, this man went down to his house justified rather than the other: for every one that exalteth himself shall be abased; and he that humbleth himself shall be exalted.

LUKE 18:9–14

∽

For I know that in me (that is, in my flesh,) dwelleth no good thing: for to will is present with me; but how to perform that which is good I find not.

ROMANS 7:18

For they being ignorant of God's righteousness, and going about to establish their own righteousness, have not submitted themselves unto the righteousness of God.

ROMANS 10:3

And be found in him, not having mine own righteousness, which is of the law, but that which is through the faith of Christ, the righteousness which is of God by faith.

PHILIPPIANS 3:9

46. ANGER AND ARGUMENTS

Even though you're doing your best to follow the Lord, you'll sometimes have to deal with feelings of anger. Or you will have to deal with others who are angry and contentious, and this isn't always easy to do.

The first thing to know about anger is that it's a valid, God-created emotion, and contrary to what some people think, it is *not* always wrong. Ephesians 4:26 advises, "Be ye angry, and sin not." The catch is, you're to be *slow* to anger and not fly off the handle quickly. "Let every man be swift to hear, slow to speak, slow to wrath" (James 1:19). The Lord Himself gets angry at times, but the Bible says He's "slow to anger" (Psalm 103:8).

Also, even godly people have strong differences of opinion, and discussions can get heated at times. One time, Paul, the apostle who wrote 1 Corinthians 13, the Love Chapter, and Barnabas, described as "a good man, and full of the Holy Ghost" (Acts 11:24), had a heated argument. "And the contention was so sharp between them, that they departed asunder one from the other" (Acts 15:39). Thankfully, they eventually worked out their differences and reconciled.

Most of the time, however, pride and a quick temper are the main causes of arguments—what the Bible calls "contentions" (Proverbs 13:10; 17:14; 18:6, 18). So avoid them.

Cease from anger, and forsake wrath: fret not thyself in any wise to do evil.

PSALM 37:8

∽

Only by pride cometh contention: but with the well advised is wisdom.

PROVERBS 13:10

∽

He that is soon angry dealeth foolishly.

PROVERBS 14:17

∽

A soft answer turneth away wrath: but grievous words stir up anger.

PROVERBS 15:1

∽

A wrathful man stirreth up strife: but he that is slow to anger appeaseth strife.

PROVERBS 15:18

∽

He that is slow to anger is better than the mighty; and he that ruleth his spirit than he that taketh a city.

PROVERBS 16:32

∽

A fool's lips enter into contention.

PROVERBS 18:6

The discretion of a man deferreth his anger; and it is his glory to pass over a transgression.

PROVERBS 19:11

∞

A gift in secret pacifieth anger: and a reward in the bosom strong wrath.

PROVERBS 21:14

∞

It is better to dwell in the wilderness, than with a contentious and an angry woman.

PROVERBS 21:19

∞

Cast out the scorner, and contention shall go out; yea, strife and reproach shall cease.

PROVERBS 22:10

∞

Make no friendship with an angry man; and with a furious man thou shalt not go.

PROVERBS 22:24

∞

Wrath is cruel, and anger is outrageous.

PROVERBS 27:4

∞

An angry man stirreth up strife, and a furious man aboundeth in transgression.

PROVERBS 29:22

Be not hasty in thy spirit to be angry: for anger resteth in the bosom of fools.

ECCLESIASTES 7:9

∞

But I say unto you, That whosoever is angry with his brother without a cause shall be in danger of the judgment: and whosoever shall say to his brother, Raca, shall be in danger of the council: but whosoever shall say, Thou fool, shall be in danger of hell fire.

MATTHEW 5:22

∞

Be ye angry, and sin not: let not the sun go down upon your wrath.

EPHESIANS 4:26

∞

Let all bitterness, and wrath, and anger, and clamour, and evil speaking, be put away from you, with all malice.

EPHESIANS 4:31

∞

But now ye also put off all these; anger, wrath, malice, blasphemy, filthy communication out of your mouth.

COLOSSIANS 3:8

∞

Forbearing one another, and forgiving one another, if any man have a quarrel against any: even as Christ forgave you, so also do ye.

COLOSSIANS 3:13

47. WISDOM

Knowledge is defined as "facts, information, and skills gained through experience or education." And *wisdom* is defined this way: "Having knowledge, experience, and good judgment, and applying it to life situations; to discern and judge properly." So knowledge is facts and information, understanding is grasping what they mean, and wisdom is the ability to use them in a beneficial way.

Job 28:28 declares, "Behold, the fear of the LORD, that is wisdom." If you want *true* wisdom, you must believe in God, love Him, be in awe of Him, and fear to disobey Him. Then, and only then, pursue knowledge.

Throughout history, God has given wisdom to men and women as an integral part of their personality. For example, in the Bible, people from Teman were well known for their wisdom; they inherited it from their parents (Jeremiah 49:7). But God has also given people downloads of wisdom and insight later in life, as He did with Solomon (1 Kings 3:4–12). God also gives many believers a spiritual gift called "the word of wisdom," divine insight on what to say or do in a specific situation (1 Corinthians 12:8; Luke 21:15).

The good news is, the Bible promises that if you lack wisdom, you can ask God for it, and He will give it to you freely (James 1:5).

And I have filled him with the spirit of God, in wisdom, and in understanding, and in knowledge, and in all manner of workmanship.

EXODUS 31:3

❧

Behold, I have taught you statutes and judgments. . . . Keep therefore and do them; for this is your wisdom and your understanding in the sight of the nations, which shall hear all these statutes, and say, Surely this great nation is a wise and understanding people.

DEUTERONOMY 4:5–6

❧

Behold, the fear of the LORD, that is wisdom; and to depart from evil is understanding.

JOB 28:28

❧

The fear of the LORD is the beginning of wisdom: a good understanding have all they that do his commandments: his praise endureth for ever.

PSALM 111:10

❧

For the LORD giveth wisdom: out of his mouth cometh knowledge and understanding.

PROVERBS 2:6

❧

Wisdom is the principal thing; therefore get wisdom: and with all thy getting get understanding.

PROVERBS 4:7

He that getteth wisdom loveth his own soul: he that keepeth understanding shall find good.

PROVERBS 19:8

∽

Wisdom strengtheneth the wise more than ten mighty men which are in the city.

ECCLESIASTES 7:19

∽

Thus saith the LORD, Let not the wise man glory in his wisdom. . .but let him that glorieth glory in this, that he understandeth and knoweth me, that I am the LORD which exercise lovingkindness, judgment, and righteousness, in the earth: for in these things I delight, saith the LORD.

JEREMIAH 9:23–24

∽

As for these four children, God gave them knowledge and skill in all learning and wisdom.

DANIEL 1:17

∽

For I will give you a mouth and wisdom, which all your adversaries shall not be able to gainsay nor resist.

LUKE 21:15

∽

For I reckon that the sufferings of this present time are not worthy to be compared with the glory which shall be revealed in us.

ROMANS 8:18

Where is the wise? where is the scribe? where is the disputer of this world? hath not God made foolish the wisdom of this world? For after that in the wisdom of God the world by wisdom knew not God, it pleased God by the foolishness of preaching to save them that believe.

1 CORINTHIANS 1:20–21

❧

And my speech and my preaching was not with enticing words of man's wisdom, but in demonstration of the Spirit and of power: that your faith should not stand in the wisdom of men, but in the power of God.

1 CORINTHIANS 2:4–5

❧

For the wisdom of this world is foolishness with God. For it is written, He taketh the wise in their own craftiness.

1 CORINTHIANS 3:19

❧

For to one is given by the Spirit the word of wisdom; to another the word of knowledge by the same Spirit.

1 CORINTHIANS 12:8

❧

That the God of our Lord Jesus Christ, the Father of glory, may give unto you the spirit of wisdom and revelation in the knowledge of him.

EPHESIANS 1:17

❧

Study to shew thyself approved unto God, a workman that needeth not to be ashamed, rightly dividing the word of truth.

2 TIMOTHY 2:15

48. SOUND SPEECH

The Bible urges believers to have "sound speech" (Titus 2:7–8) and "a wholesome tongue" (Proverbs 15:4). It says, "The words of a wise man's mouth are gracious," and they "minister grace unto the hearers" (Ecclesiastes 10:12; Ephesians 4:29). It also tells us that a wise woman "openeth her mouth with wisdom; and in her tongue is the law of kindness" (Proverbs 31:26).

God's Word declares that "the mouth of a righteous man is a well of life" (Proverbs 10:11). Picture a person drawing water from deep within a well and pouring it over the lip of the well, bringing refreshment and life to others. If the heart is right, the words that flow out of it will be wholesome.

In stark contrast, "the mouth of the wicked speaketh frowardness [crooked, perverse things]" (Proverbs 10:32). Ecclesiastes describes the end result of an uncontrolled tongue: "The beginning of the words of his mouth is foolishness: and the end of his talk is mischievous madness" (Ecclesiastes 10:13).

This is why God instructs Christians to avoid "filthiness, foolish talking, and jesting," as well as "vain babblings" (see Ephesians 5:4; 1 Timothy 6:20). Paul wrote, "Let no corrupt communication proceed out of your mouth, but that which is good to the use of edifying" (Ephesians 4:29). Speak things that build people up, instead of tearing them down.

Thou shalt not go up and down as a talebearer among thy people.

LEVITICUS 19:16

∽

But I would strengthen you with my mouth, and the moving of my lips should asswage your grief.

JOB 16:5

∽

They that seek my hurt speak mischievous things, and imagine deceits all the day long.

PSALM 38:12

∽

Come and hear, all ye that fear God, and I will declare what he hath done for my soul.

PSALM 66:16

∽

Put away from thee a froward mouth, and perverse lips put far from thee.

PROVERBS 4:24

∽

All the words of my mouth are in righteousness; there is nothing froward or perverse in them.

PROVERBS 8:8

∽

The mouth of a righteous man is a well of life: but violence covereth the mouth of the wicked.

PROVERBS 10:11

The lips of the righteous know what is acceptable: but the mouth of the wicked speaketh frowardness.

PROVERBS 10:32

∞

A talebearer revealeth secrets: but he that is of a faithful spirit concealeth the matter.

PROVERBS 11:13

∞

A man hath joy by the answer of his mouth: and a word spoken in due season, how good is it!

PROVERBS 15:23

∞

Pleasant words are as an honeycomb, sweet to the soul, and health to the bones.

PROVERBS 16:24

∞

The words of a talebearer are as wounds, and they go down into the innermost parts of the belly.

PROVERBS 18:8

∞

He that goeth about as a talebearer revealeth secrets: therefore meddle not with him that flattereth with his lips.

PROVERBS 20:19

∞

Look not thou upon the wine. . . . At the last it biteth like a serpent, and stingeth like an adder. Thine eyes shall behold strange women, and thine heart shall utter perverse things.

PROVERBS 23:31–33

*As a mad man who casteth firebrands, arrows, and death,
so is the man that deceiveth his neighbour, and saith, Am
not I in sport?*

PROVERBS 26:18–19

*She openeth her mouth with wisdom; and in her tongue is
the law of kindness.*

PROVERBS 31:26

*The words of a wise man's mouth are gracious; but the lips
of a fool will swallow up himself. The beginning of the
words of his mouth is foolishness: and the end of his talk is
mischievous madness.*

ECCLESIASTES 10:12–13

*The Lord GOD hath given me the tongue of the learned,
that I should know how to speak a word in season to him
that is weary.*

ISAIAH 50:4

*Let no corrupt communication proceed out of your mouth,
but that which is good to the use of edifying, that it may
minister grace unto the hearers.*

EPHESIANS 4:29

*Neither filthiness, nor foolish talking, nor jesting, which
are not convenient: but rather giving of thanks.*

EPHESIANS 5:4

49. HONESTY AND INTEGRITY

The apostle Paul wrote that Christians are to strive to "lead a quiet and peaceable life in all godliness and honesty" (1 Timothy 2:2). You are also to be *valiant* for the truth. God said that those who "are not valiant for the truth. . .know not me" (Jeremiah 9:3). Moreover, you are to be a person with "an honest and good heart" (Luke 8:15).

Integrity is closely related to honesty. A dictionary definition for *integrity* is "the quality of being honest and having strong moral principles; moral uprightness." Another related word is *just*, as in "a just weight" or "the just"—referring to honest, fair, and righteous people.

Regarding "a just weight," in ancient Israel, merchants sold grain, food, and so on by weight on a pair of balances. There were standard weights for the various stones used, and merchants' stones were to match these standards. "A just weight and balance are the LORD's" (Proverbs 16:11). Dishonest merchants had accurate weights they used for favored clients, but lighter stones they pulled out to defraud others.

Another place people's honesty was put to the test was whether they told the truth or "bore false witness" in a court of law. This was so important it was one of the Ten Commandments: "Thou shalt not bear false witness against thy neighbour" (Exodus 20:16).

Thou shalt not raise a false report: put not thine hand with the wicked to be an unrighteous witness.

EXODUS 23:1

Just balances, just weights, a just ephah, and a just hin, shall ye have: I am the LORD your God.

LEVITICUS 19:36

Thou shalt not have in thy bag divers weights, a great and a small. Thou shalt not have in thine house divers measures, a great and a small. But thou shalt have a perfect and just weight, a perfect and just measure shalt thou have: that thy days may be lengthened in the land which the LORD thy God giveth thee.

DEUTERONOMY 25:13–15

Let integrity and uprightness preserve me; for I wait on thee.

PSALM 25:21

Let the lying lips be put to silence; which speak grievous things proudly and contemptuously against the righteous.

PSALM 31:18

I hate and abhor lying: but thy law do I love.

PSALM 119:163

The curse of the LORD is in the house of the wicked: but he blesseth the habitation of the just.

PROVERBS 3:33

∞

He that hideth hatred with lying lips, and he that uttereth a slander, is a fool.

PROVERBS 10:18

∞

A false balance is abomination to the LORD: but a just weight is his delight.

PROVERBS 11:1

∞

The integrity of the upright shall guide them.

PROVERBS 11:3

∞

The lip of truth shall be established for ever: but a lying tongue is but for a moment.

PROVERBS 12:19

∞

A faithful witness will not lie: but a false witness will utter lies.

PROVERBS 14:5

∞

The just man walketh in his integrity: his children are blessed after him.

PROVERBS 20:7

A lying tongue hateth those that are afflicted by it; and a flattering mouth worketh ruin.

PROVERBS 26:28

The way of the just is uprightness: thou, most upright, dost weigh the path of the just.

ISAIAH 26:7

These are the things that ye shall do; Speak ye every man the truth to his neighbour; execute the judgment of truth and peace in your gates.

ZECHARIAH 8:16

Jesus said unto them. . .Ye are of your father the devil, and the lusts of your father ye will do. He was a murderer from the beginning, and abode not in the truth, because there is no truth in him. When he speaketh a lie, he speaketh of his own: for he is a liar, and the father of it.

JOHN 8:42, 44

Wherefore, brethren, look ye out among you seven men of honest report, full of the Holy Ghost and wisdom, whom we may appoint over this business.

ACTS 6:3

Provide things honest in the sight of all men.

ROMANS 12:17

50. SEXUAL MORALITY

In the Western world—in North America in particular—the media constantly bombards society with images and talk of sexual immorality and lasciviousness, in movies, in TV shows, and in advertising. This steady barrage of permissiveness has so permeated modern society that it's now considered the norm, and Christians who advocate sexual continence and refrain from "free sex" are considered old-fashioned and puritanical.

God is the one who dreamed up sex, designed men's and women's bodies, and built a longing for physical intimacy into their DNA. He ensured the very survival of the human species by tying it to sexual desire. His very first commandment to Adam and Eve was "Be fruitful, and multiply" (Genesis 1:28).

But God insists that men and women enjoy such intimacy within the bounds of marriage. This is still His standard. It hasn't changed.

How can you keep the steady stream of sexual immorality from eroding your foundations? Take a stand against it in your heart, first of all. Job explained, "I made a covenant with mine eyes" (Job 31:1). He determined ahead of time, before he was even faced with temptation, to refuse to "think upon a maid" with desire and lust. If even the great, righteous patriarch Job found it necessary to take a strong mental stand in this area, you should too.

And it came to pass after these things, that his master's wife cast her eyes upon Joseph; and she said, Lie with me. But he refused, and said unto his master's wife. . .There is none greater in this house than I; neither hath he kept back any thing from me but thee, because thou art his wife: how then can I do this great wickedness, and sin against God? And it came to pass, as she spake to Joseph day by day, that he hearkened not unto her, to lie by her, or to be with her. And it came to pass about this time, that Joseph went into the house to do his business; and there was none of the men of the house there within. And she caught him by his garment, saying, Lie with me: and he left his garment in her hand, and fled, and got him out.

GENESIS 39:7–12

∞

I made a covenant with mine eyes; why then should I think upon a maid?

JOB 31:1

∞

Lust not after her beauty in thine heart; neither let her take thee with her eyelids.

PROVERBS 6:25

∞

With her much fair speech she caused him to yield, with the flattering of her lips she forced him. He goeth after her straightway, as an ox goeth to the slaughter, or as a fool to the correction of the stocks; till a dart strike through his liver; as a bird hasteth to the snare, and knoweth not that it is for his life.

PROVERBS 7:21–23

Ye have heard that it was said by them of old time, Thou shalt not commit adultery: but I say unto you, That whosoever looketh on a woman to lust after her hath committed adultery with her already in his heart.

MATTHEW 5:27–28

Flee fornication. Every sin that a man doeth is without the body; but he that committeth fornication sinneth against his own body.

1 CORINTHIANS 6:18

Having a form of godliness, but denying the power thereof: from such turn away. For of this sort are they which creep into houses, and lead captive silly women laden with sins, led away with divers lusts.

2 TIMOTHY 3:5–6

The Lord knoweth how to deliver the godly out of temptations, and to reserve the unjust unto the day of judgment to be punished: but chiefly them that walk after the flesh in the lust of uncleanness. . . . Having eyes full of adultery, and that cannot cease from sin; beguiling unstable souls. . . . For when they speak great swelling words of vanity, they allure through the lusts of the flesh, through much wantonness, those that were clean escaped from them who live in error.

2 PETER 2:9–10, 14, 18

Marriage is honourable in all, and the bed undefiled: but whoremongers and adulterers God will judge.

HEBREWS 13:4

∞

For there are certain men crept in unawares, who were before of old ordained to this condemnation, ungodly men, turning the grace of our God into lasciviousness.

JUDE 1:4

∞

But I have a few things against thee, because thou hast there them that hold the doctrine of Balaam, who taught Balac to cast a stumblingblock before the children of Israel. . .to commit fornication.

REVELATION 2:14

∞

Notwithstanding I have a few things against thee, because thou sufferest that woman Jezebel, which calleth herself a prophetess, to teach and to seduce my servants to commit fornication.

REVELATION 2:20

51. MARRIAGE

In Bible times, as today, weddings were festive, joyful occasions. Four times the prophet Jeremiah repeats the phrase "the voice of joy, and the voice of gladness, the voice of the bridegroom, and the voice of the bride" (Jeremiah 33:11). And Isaiah declares, "As the bridegroom rejoiceth over the bride, so shall thy God rejoice over thee" (Isaiah 62:5).

Marriage is a blessed estate, made all the more blessed by the rapturous pleasures a husband and wife enjoy within that union. First Corinthians 7:3, which in the King James Version reads, "Let the husband render unto the wife due benevolence: and likewise also the wife unto the husband," literally means for them to fulfill each other's desire for sexual intimacy. Proverbs 5:18–19 says, "Let thy fountain be blessed: and rejoice with the wife of thy youth. . .and be thou ravished always with her love."

And such intimacy leads directly to the joy of having children! Malachi 2:15 says, "And did not he make [them] one? . . . And wherefore one? That he might seek a godly seed." Psalm 127:4–5 promises, "As arrows are in the hand of a mighty man; so are children of the youth. Happy is the man that hath his quiver full of them."

And finally, marriage is intended to provide lifelong union with another person and to provide security and a bedrock of trust.

Let thy fountain be blessed: and rejoice with the wife of thy youth. Let her be as the loving hind and pleasant roe; let her breasts satisfy thee at all times; and be thou ravished always with her love.

PROVERBS 5:18–19

For as. . .the bridegroom rejoiceth over the bride, so shall thy God rejoice over thee.

ISAIAH 62:5

It is good for a man not to touch a woman. Nevertheless, to avoid fornication, let every man have his own wife, and let every woman have her own husband. Let the husband render unto the wife due benevolence: and likewise also the wife unto the husband. The wife hath not power of her own body, but the husband: and likewise also the husband hath not power of his own body, but the wife. Defraud ye not one the other, except it be with consent for a time, that ye may give yourselves to fasting and prayer; and come together again, that Satan tempt you not for your incontinency.

1 CORINTHIANS 7:1–5

But if they cannot contain, let them marry: for it is better to marry than to burn.

1 CORINTHIANS 7:9

Marriage is honourable in all, and the bed undefiled: but whoremongers and adulterers God will judge.

HEBREWS 13:4

*He that is unmarried careth for the things that belong
to the Lord, how he may please the Lord: but he that is
married careth for the things that are of the world, how he
may please his wife. There is difference also between a wife
and a virgin. The unmarried woman careth for the things
of the Lord. . .but she that is married careth for the things
of the world, how she may please her husband.*

1 CORINTHIANS 7:32–34

∞

*Wives, submit yourselves unto your own husbands, as unto
the Lord. For the husband is the head of the wife, even as
Christ is the head of the church: and he is the saviour of the
body. Therefore as the church is subject unto Christ, so let
the wives be to their own husbands in every thing.*

EPHESIANS 5:22–24

∞

*Husbands, love your wives, even as Christ also loved the
church, and gave himself for it. . . . So ought men to love
their wives as their own bodies. He that loveth his wife
loveth himself.*

EPHESIANS 5:25, 28

∞

*That every one of you should know how to possess his
vessel in sanctification and honour; not in the lust of
concupiscence, even as the Gentiles which know not God:
that no man go beyond and defraud his brother in any
matter: because that the Lord is the avenger of all such,
as we also have forewarned you and testified.*

1 THESSALONIANS 4:4–6

The wife is bound by the law as long as her husband liveth; but if her husband be dead, she is at liberty to be married to whom she will; only in the Lord.

1 Corinthians 7:39

Likewise, ye wives, be in subjection to your own husbands; that, if any obey not the word, they also may without the word be won by the conversation [lifestyle] of the wives; while they behold your chaste conversation coupled with fear.

1 Peter 3:1–2

Likewise, ye husbands, dwell with them according to knowledge, giving honour unto the wife, as unto the weaker vessel, and as being heirs together of the grace of life; that your prayers be not hindered.

1 Peter 3:7

52. RAISING CHILDREN

Children are a tremendous blessing, but they're also a great responsibility. When God gives you sons and daughters, He's trusting them to your care. While your extended family and church family can help mold their lives, it's primarily your responsibility to pass on God's Word to them, to teach them to worship Him, and to instill godly character in them. How they respond to their upbringing is ultimately their choice, but you must lead them.

The Bible speaks often about disciplining children, but it also reveals the gentle side of child-rearing. Paul said to his converts, "Ye know how we exhorted and comforted and charged every one of you, as a father doth his children" (1 Thessalonians 2:11). Even corrective discipline should be motivated by deep love, "for whom the LORD loveth he correcteth; even as a father the son in whom he delighteth" (Proverbs 3:12).

Children can bring you great joy, but they can also bring you tears and times of grief. Jesus spoke of two fathers who each had two sons, and His teaching reveals that rebellious attitudes, laziness, and youthful waywardness are not new (see Matthew 21:28–31; Luke 15:11–13). But it also reveals a parent's undying love for his or her children (Luke 15:20). And that's one thing you must have to be a parent: unconditional love.

And these words, which I command thee this day, shall be in thine heart: and thou shalt teach them diligently unto thy children, and shalt talk of them when thou sittest in thine house, and when thou walkest by the way, and when thou liest down, and when thou risest up.

DEUTERONOMY 6:6–7

∞

My son, if thou wilt receive my words, and hide my commandments with thee; so that thou incline thine ear unto wisdom, and apply thine heart to understanding.

PROVERBS 2:1–2

∞

My son, despise not the chastening of the LORD; neither be weary of his correction: for whom the LORD loveth he correcteth; even as a father the son in whom he delighteth.

PROVERBS 3:11–12

∞

My son, keep thy father's commandment, and forsake not the law of thy mother.

PROVERBS 6:20

∞

Now therefore hearken unto me, O ye children: for blessed are they that keep my ways.

PROVERBS 8:32

∞

A good man leaveth an inheritance to his children's children: and the wealth of the sinner is laid up for the just.

PROVERBS 13:22

He that spareth his rod hateth his son: but he that loveth him chasteneth him betimes.

PROVERBS 13:24

∽

Chasten thy son while there is hope, and let not thy soul spare for his crying.

PROVERBS 19:18

∽

The just man walketh in his integrity: his children are blessed after him.

PROVERBS 20:7

∽

Correct thy son, and he shall give thee rest; yea, he shall give delight unto thy soul.

PROVERBS 29:17

∽

She looketh well to the ways of her household, and eateth not the bread of idleness. Her children arise up, and call her blessed.

PROVERBS 31:27–28

∽

A certain man had two sons; and he came to the first, and said, Son, go work to day in my vineyard. He answered and said, I will not: but afterward he repented, and went. And he came to the second, and said likewise. And he answered and said, I go, sir: and went not. Whether of them twain did the will of his father? They say unto him, The first.

MATTHEW 21:28–31

A certain man had two sons: and the younger of them said to his father, Father, give me the portion of goods that falleth to me. And he divided unto them his living. And not many days after the younger son gathered all together, and took his journey into a far country, and there wasted his substance with riotous living.

LUKE 15:11–13

∞

Children, obey your parents in the Lord: for this is right. Honour thy father and mother; which is the first commandment with promise; that it may be well with thee, and thou mayest live long on the earth. And, ye fathers, provoke not your children to wrath: but bring them up in the nurture and admonition of the Lord.

EPHESIANS 6:1–4

∞

Fathers, provoke not your children to anger, lest they be discouraged.

COLOSSIANS 3:21

∞

But if any provide not for his own, and specially for those of his own house, he hath denied the faith, and is worse than an infidel.

1 TIMOTHY 5:8

∞

But continue thou in the things which thou hast learned and hast been assured of, knowing of whom thou hast learned them; and that from a child thou hast known the holy scriptures, which are able to make thee wise unto salvation through faith which is in Christ Jesus.

2 TIMOTHY 3:14–15

53. HEALING

When talking about God's healing power, it's important to find a balance. You must have faith in the many healing promises in God's Word, yet not be presumptuous and insist that God *must* heal in any given circumstance.

People often end up in one of two extremes: they read God's many wonderful healing promises and then, when faced with a chronic illness in themselves or a loved one, begin to claim these promises. Far too often, however, they treat God's Word like a contract. This degenerates into a "name it and claim it" attitude.

However, despite their insistence, they or their loved ones frequently aren't healed. So they become disillusioned and give up trusting God. They then look exclusively to modern medicine or natural healing methods such as diets of raw vegetables and fruits. These can provide many benefits, but many medical conditions are still beyond human help.

What are you to do? By all means, avail yourself of both modern and natural healing methods *and* have faith in God's promises. Pray sincerely and in faith. Submit yourself and your body into the hands of your loving Creator—and pray that He gives you the faith for a miracle, big or small. You can't just *try* to have faith. God must stir up such faith in your heart.

*If thou wilt diligently hearken to the voice of the LORD thy
God, and wilt do that which is right in his sight, and wilt
give ear to his commandments, and keep all his statutes,
I will put none of these diseases upon thee, which I have
brought upon the Egyptians: for I am the LORD that
healeth thee.*

EXODUS 15:26

∞

*And the LORD will take away from thee all sickness, and
will put none of the evil diseases of Egypt, which thou
knowest, upon thee.*

DEUTERONOMY 7:15

∞

*Thus saith the LORD, the God of David thy father, I have
heard thy prayer, I have seen thy tears: behold, I will heal
thee. . . . And Isaiah said, Take a lump of figs. And they
took and laid it on the boil, and he recovered.*

2 KINGS 20:5, 7

∞

*And Asa in the thirty and ninth year of his reign was
diseased in his feet, until his disease was exceeding great:
yet in his disease he sought not to the LORD, but to the
physicians. And Asa. . .died in the one and fortieth year of
his reign.*

2 CHRONICLES 16:12–13

∞

*Bless the LORD, O my soul, and forget not all his benefits: who
forgiveth all thine iniquities; who healeth all thy diseases.*

PSALM 103:2–3

Who satisfieth thy mouth with good things; so that thy youth is renewed like the eagle's.

PSALM 103:5

∞

He sent his word, and healed them, and delivered them from their destructions.

PSALM 107:20

∞

Come, and let us return unto the LORD*: for he hath torn, and he will heal us; he hath smitten, and he will bind us up.*

HOSEA 6:1

∞

But unto you that fear my name shall the Sun of righteousness arise with healing in his wings.

MALACHI 4:2

∞

When the even was come, they brought unto him many that were possessed with devils: and he cast out the spirits with his word, and healed all that were sick: that it might be fulfilled which was spoken by Esaias the prophet, saying, Himself took our infirmities, and bare our sicknesses.

MATTHEW 8:16–17

∞

But when Jesus knew it, he withdrew himself from thence: and great multitudes followed him, and he healed them all.

MATTHEW 12:15

They that be whole need not a physician, but they that are sick.

MATTHEW 9:12

Therefore I say unto you, What things soever ye desire, when ye pray, believe that ye receive them, and ye shall have them.

MARK 11:24

And these signs shall follow them that believe. . .they shall lay hands on the sick, and they shall recover.

MARK 16:17–18

Peter said unto him, Aeneas, Jesus Christ maketh thee whole: arise, and make thy bed. And he arose immediately.

ACTS 9:34

But the manifestation of the Spirit is given to every man to profit withal. For to one is given. . .faith by the same Spirit; to another the gifts of healing by the same Spirit.

1 CORINTHIANS 12:7–9

Is any sick among you? let him call for the elders of the church; and let them pray over him, anointing him with oil in the name of the Lord: and the prayer of faith shall save the sick, and the Lord shall raise him up; and if he have committed sins, they shall be forgiven him.

JAMES 5:14–15

54. HOPE OF HEAVEN

As a Christian, you have a wonderful hope of heaven, eternal life in the presence of a glorious, loving God, that you'll enjoy after this life. Paul wrote in AD 55, "Eye hath not seen, nor ear heard, neither have entered into the heart of man, the things which God hath prepared for them that love him" (1 Corinthians 2:9). But in AD 97, some forty-two years later, God gave a fantastic look at heaven that has thrilled followers of Christ ever since.

Even with that, however, Christians still have been given only a glimpse of heaven. It's one thing to read about heaven in the Bible; it will be quite another to actually *experience* the rapturous ecstasy of God's celestial city firsthand. And it's real and tangible. Heaven isn't just an endless landscape of cumulus clouds and light where you drift for eternity, feeling joy.

Heaven is a real place! The capital of heaven is the New Jerusalem, an astonishing city in another dimension. And what's more, after the thousand-year reign of Christ on this physical planet, the earth will be melted and re-formed into a global Eden, and God's celestial city will descend out of the spiritual dimension and be on earth forever.

You'll walk the golden streets of that city with your saved loved ones forever. That will truly be heaven!

In my Father's house are many mansions: if it were not so, I would have told you. I go to prepare a place for you. And if I go and prepare a place for you, I will come again, and receive you unto myself; that where I am, there ye may be also.

JOHN 14:2–3

∞

Eye hath not seen, nor ear heard, neither have entered into the heart of man, the things which God hath prepared for them that love him.

1 CORINTHIANS 2:9

∞

For ye. . .took joyfully the spoiling of your goods, knowing in yourselves that ye have in heaven a better and an enduring substance.

HEBREWS 10:34

∞

But now they desire a better country, that is, an heavenly: wherefore God is not ashamed to be called their God: for he hath prepared for them a city.

HEBREWS 11:16

∞

But ye are come unto mount Sion, and unto the city of the living God, the heavenly Jerusalem, and to an innumerable company of angels, to the general assembly and church of the firstborn, which are written in heaven, and to God the Judge of all, and to the spirits of just men made perfect.

HEBREWS 12:22–23

After this I beheld, and, lo, a great multitude, which no
man could number, of all nations, and kindreds, and
people, and tongues, stood before the throne, and before the
Lamb, clothed with white robes. . . . Therefore are they
before the throne of God, and serve him day and night in
his temple: and he that sitteth on the throne shall dwell
among them. They shall hunger no more, neither thirst any
more; neither shall the sun light on them, nor any heat.
For the Lamb which is in the midst of the throne shall feed
them, and shall lead them unto living fountains of waters:
and God shall wipe away all tears from their eyes.

REVELATION 7:9, 15–17

∞

And God shall wipe away all tears from their eyes; and
there shall be no more death, neither sorrow, nor crying,
neither shall there be any more pain: for the former things
are passed away.

REVELATION 21:4

∞

And he carried me away in the spirit to a great and
high mountain, and shewed me that great city, the holy
Jerusalem, descending out of heaven from God, having
the glory of God: and her light was like unto a stone
most precious, even like a jasper stone, clear as crystal.

REVELATION 21:10–11

∞

Blessed are they that do his commandments, that they may
have right to the tree of life, and may enter in through the
gates into the city.

REVELATION 22:14

nd the building of the wall of it was of jasper: and the city
as pure gold, like unto clear glass. And the foundations
f the wall of the city were garnished with all manner of
recious stones. . . . And the twelve gates were twelve pearls:
very several gate was of one pearl: and the street of the city
as pure gold, as it were transparent glass.

REVELATION 21:18–19, 21

nd he shewed me a pure river of water of life, clear as
rystal, proceeding out of the throne of God and of the
amb. In the midst of the street of it, and on either side
f the river, was there the tree of life, which bare twelve
nanner of fruits, and yielded her fruit every month: and
he leaves of the tree were for the healing of the nations.

REVELATION 22:1–2

Special Editions of
The Bible Promise Book®

*The Bible Promise Book®
Devotional*

For more than thirty years, *The Bible Promise Book®* has blessed millions of readers. Now this brand-new daily devotional highlights more than forty *Bible Promise Book®* topics from A to Z—from Adversity and Gratitude to Forgiveness, Patience, Salvation, and Wisdom. Perfect for daily quiet time or Bible study, *The Bible Promise Book® Devotional* is perfect for readers of all ages.
Paperback / 978-1-68322-181-4 / $7.99

The Bible Promise Book® for Men

The Bible Promise Book® for Men is a compilation of hundreds of Bible verses, categorized under dozens of key life topics. Drawing from varied Bible translations for ease of reading, this book features subjects such as Brothers, Competitiveness, Emotions, Exercise, Fatherhood, Leadership, Legacy, Mentoring, Service, Sports, and Temptation.
DiCarta / 978-1-68322-186-9 / $15.99